Creating Stories

By Hank Quense

Other books by Hank Quense

Fiction:

Princess Moxie

Moxie's Problem

Moxie's Decision

Princess Moxie

Gundarland Stories

Tales From Gundarland

Falstaff's Big Gamble

Wotan's Dilemma

The King Who Disappeared

Zaftan Trilogy

Zaftan Entrepreneurs

Zaftan Miscreants

Non-fiction:

Complete self-publishing Guides

Planning a Novel, Script or Memoir

Manage Your Story Design Project

License Notes

ISBN: 978-0-997822458
Published in the United States of America.
Published by Strange Worlds Publishing
http://strangeworldspublishing.com/wp

Acknowledgements

While I wrote the book, other people provided a considerable amount of work that was necessary to whip it into shape. An early version was read and commented on by Nancy Taiani, Helen Lippman and Eileen Conte. The final editing was done by Martha Moffet. All of these women (and I) are members of the Write Group that meets in the library at Montclair NJ.

Table of Contents

Foreword

If you're reading this book, you must have an interest in writing a story. What kind of story doesn't matter. Whether you intend to write a short story, a play, a script, a novel or even a memoir, this book will help you get it done.

"How can that be?" you ask. Simply because a novel, a script, a memoir, a play, a short story are all stories. And no matter what type of story you have in mind, each needs a set of common elements such as characters, plots, scenes, settings, character arcs and more.

The only difference between the types of stories listed above is the output. What the manuscript looks like, in other words. The manuscripts for a novel and a play will look very different, but the process of producing the manuscripts is exactly the same.

If you skim the book you'll see a lot of material, perhaps a daunting amount of material. If you're a beginning writer, don't panic; you don't have to master all the material in one bite. The best approach is to concentrate on one aspect at a time in your writing. Once you've become adept at that aspect try another one. To begin, I'd recommend focusing on character building. Second, master scene design. After that, go where your curiosity takes you.

Let's put that issue aside and dive right in. Stories are the result of three separate creative processes:

> Creative ideas
> Story design
> Storytelling techniques

I can't help an author with the ideas, but this book is about the last two, the story design process and storytelling.

This book is primarily aimed at the writer trying to master the craft of writing stories and telling those stories in a way that will hold the reader's attention. It will also be useful to experienced writers as a refresher course to correct the slovenly writing habits that we all fall into over time. This includes me. I'm constantly searching for (and finding!) defective writing habits that I have developed over time.

The premise behind this book is that stories don't pop into the author's head fully formed. Another premise is that one can't write a story from a single idea. Creating a story requires the author to come up with a number of ideas and then package those ideas inside the story.

The author needs ideas on characters, plot events, setting and scene design to mention a few areas. Coming up with all these story ideas is easier for some people and harder for others. Thus, a story is the product of many hours of patient work on the different facets that are needed to build a compelling story. In some cases, you may spend as much time in thinking as you do in writing. This is especially true in the design stages of the project.

What is story design? To me, it's the process of developing all the story elements, characters, plot events and so forth before beginning the storytelling process. Only after I've completed all the design work will I start writing the first draft. More about that later. In the case of my novel — *Falstaff's Big Gamble* — the story design work took three months. Only after that time did I start to write the first draft.

Story design and storytelling techniques are much more important than the ability to write well. That sounds blasphemous, doesn't it? The fact is, editors and publishers don't buy stories because they are well-written. Editors and publishers buy stories that have superior story design and utilize storytelling techniques. If that story also happens to be well-written, that is a bonus, but it won't enter into the "buy" decision.

I'm sure some people will claim I am stifling creativity by offering a design process. I disagree. Nothing in my process stifles creativity; rather my process channels creative ideas so that more time is available to the author to be creative. I realize the process I describe won't satisfy every writer. Many of them will feel they can't get their mind to adapt to my way of working through a story design. That's cool. For them, I say take whatever you find practical and use it. Ignore the rest.

Some of the issues addressed in this book are the ones that books and manuals on writing either gloss over or explain using a wealth of technical-sounding gibberish. My approach uses plain language and gives simple examples to explain these concepts.

This book layout involves four parts. Part 1 discusses story setting and character development. Part 2 deals with plots and scene design. Part 3 is all about storytelling techniques. Topics included are point of view, foreshadowing, stimulus and reaction and other topics. Part 4 contains stuff that doesn't fit neatly into the other parts. These include writing humor and satire, writing software, mind-maps and other topics.

If you have specific questions about the material in this book, you can email me at hanque (at) verizon (dot) net and I'll try to answer them.

~ ~ ~

This book is dedicated to all the many writers who taught me how to create stories by critiquing my early, pathetic attempts to write a short story.

Part 1: Setting and Characters

Chapter 1: Getting Started

Hank Quense: To begin with, let's discuss a few preliminary concepts and ideas.

Author: What? Never mind this nebulous garbage. Let's get into the good stuff.

HQ: You need to understand a few things first.

Author: I need to know about characters and plots.

HQ: Hey! Who's writing this book? You or me?

Author: You.

HQ: That's right. And I have stuff I have to discuss with you.

Author: All right. We'll do it your way.

HQ: Thanks. Now that we've settled that issue, let's move on to the ideas and concepts I want to tell you about.

Beginning Thoughts

Do you have a story to write? A story consists of several mandatory design elements. There are also a number of storytelling techniques that modern readers expect to see in the story.

This book concentrates on those two areas: story design and storytelling.

So, what is a story? Let's agree on a definition. I like these two definitions by two different and very prolific authors.

A story is a narrative description of a character struggling to solve a problem. Nothing more than that. And nothing less. Ben Bova *The Craft of Writing Science Fiction*.

A story consists of a character in a context with a problem. Based on Algis Budrys's book *Writing to the Point*.

Both of these statements say essentially the same thing. The key elements are: character, struggle, problem, context (setting).

I find it interesting that the definitions say "story" but don't mention what type of story such as a novel or a script. The reason for that is that the type of story is irrelevant. A story is a story. The definition applies to any and all types of stories since all types of stories require characters, plots, setting, scenes and other elements.

The only difference between a novel and a script is the way the manuscript looks. Formatting a novel is much different from formatting a script.

The only difference between a novel and a memoir is that one is fictional and one is not fictional.

These definitions above are what I will use in describing the various elements in story design and storytelling. Stories are about characters. If your story concerns itself with events, it's history, even if the history is made up. Stories are about how the characters react to those events not about the events themselves.

Before we get too far into the book, I should explain that there are two types of authors: planners and pantsters. Planners — and I'm one of these — plan everything out in advance. Pantsters — those who fly by the seat of their pants — don't believe in planning. They jump in and start writing and are always surprised by the ending.

If you're a pantster, you still have to develop characters and scenes even if the plot hatches along the way to the climax. This means that some of the material in this book will be pertinent to you. Other parts, not so much since you don't do planning.

Writing the first draft

So, you get this great story idea. You jump in front of your computer and you start writing the first scene. As you type away, you're thinking, "Wow! This will be my best story ever." You finish the first scene and start on the second one still pumped up. After a thousand or fifteen hundred words, you run out of gas. You stare at the screen and wonder, "What happened? Where is the great story I thought I had?"

What happened is you started to write a story from a single idea. That will never work. A short story needs at least five or six good ideas. A longer work like a novel requires more than a hundred. You need ideas about plot events. You need ideas about characters. You need ideas about the story setting and about story events. You need ideas about scene setting. You need ideas about character arcs, emotional arcs, and myriad other elements.

The key question here is when do you start writing the first draft?

Let's look at this from a different perspective. For purposes of this analysis, we'll say the total amount of work involved in developing the story design is represented by the circle below.

This work includes all the design work and writing the first draft. Of the total amount of work involved in producing that first draft, the actual writing of that draft is about fifteen percent of the total and it has to be the last fifteen percent, not the first.

Starting the first draft as soon as a story idea occurs is a common mistake beginning writers make. It takes experience and patience to step back and design the story before attempting to write the draft.

Another way of looking at this is to consider the story as a new house. Before you can move in, the foundation has to be in place so the walls and roof can be raised. The building shell has to have electrical and plumbing work done. The walls have to be sheet-rocked and windows installed. Appliances have to delivered and installed. The walls have to be painted. Only after all this work is done can you lay the rugs and move in the furniture.

All this construction work is the equivalent of the story's design work, while moving in the furniture is the first draft.

Granted, this isn't easy to do, especially the first time you attempt to write a story this way. Writing the first draft as the last activity is counter-intuitive. Otherwise everyone would do it without needing to read a book on writing.

Author Limitations

It may come as a surprise to new writers that as you develop a story, you place limitations on what you can do as an author. The development process also places limits on what the characters can do and not do.

Essentially, the limitations are the result of your development of the story because you have created a fictional world and that world has rules. You have to follow these rules or the reader will smoke out your rule-breaking and stop reading.

For instance, suppose your story takes place in a castle during Medieval days. Once the reader understands this setting she also understands the rules that apply to your story. Since the world in your story is Medieval, it follows that your story must stick to the Medieval era conditions. You can't have a character running around with a Derringer pistol concealed up his sleeve. You can't have a character use quantum mechanics to solve a problem.

If a character has a scrawny build, you can't have that character pick up a heavy boulder to throw at another character. Unless, of course, your character has superpowers. If your character is an optimist, you can't have her bad-mouthing everyone's suggestions; that's how a pessimist would react, not an optimist.

If your story is set in the future on a space ship exploring other galaxies, you can't use twentieth century technologies to power the ship or to communicate. It just won't work with the readers (or the publishers).

Once you've fully developed the characters, the setting, the plot and the character arc, you will be amazed at how many limitations you've placed on yourself.

Images

A story must involve the reader. The reader's job is to make mental images of the setting, the characters, the actions and other aspects of the story. The reader does this by using the author's words to form those images. This implies that the author's job is to provide the necessary words to allow the reader to come up with those images.

If the author doesn't supply the necessary words, the reader will arbitrarily build her own images independent of the author. If the author, later in the story, gets around to providing the description and the reader discovers her images were wrong, she will not be amused.

Thus, part of the author's mandate is to describe the characters so the reader can build a picture of the character. If the reader's idea about what the character looks like doesn't match the author's image, it is not a problem. Once the reader latches onto the story, it becomes hers and the story no longer belongs to the author. Whatever images the reader builds concerning the characters, they are *her* images and those images become part of the reader's story.

Similarly, the story setting and scene settings must be described so the reader can build up a store of these images. The same principle applies to action scenes. The author must provide the reader with sufficient details so she can follow the action and picture what is happening.

Developing these images is one of the biggest differences between reading a story and watching a movie or a TV show. Reading requires the use of the brain; movies and TV shows do not. TV and movies provide all the necessary imagery the viewer needs. The viewer sees the characters and their clothes. She sees the setting. She sees the action. No brain work is required. All she has to do is switch off the brain and enjoy the show.

I prefer reading and building my own images, which is why I rarely watch TV or a movie. I read books instead.

Here is an outgrowth of this image building. How many times have you heard someone say, "Loved the book, hated the movie?" I suspect that a primary reason for this love-hate reaction is that the reader went to the movie with a set of preconceived images developed from reading the book. The director, meanwhile, developed a different set of images and the director's images didn't agree with the reader's images.

The point of this discussion is that readers need to develop their own images in order to enjoy the story and that means an author has a responsibility to provide those image words.

Don't disappoint them.

How Many Characters?

Is there such a thing as too many or too few characters? This is a question that each writer has to face up to with each new story. Let's divide up the characters into three categories. The first one is for the main characters, the second for major characters and the third for minor characters.

The main characters consist of the protagonist, the hero, the antagonist, or bad guy, and a sidekick for the hero A sidekick for the bad guy is optional, but useful. It is a basic story requirement that the cast have both a protagonist and an antagonist. The story can have more than one of each, but it must have at least one of each.

The major characters are less important than the main characters, but still important to the story. They could be, for instance, the people who work with or who support one of the main characters. These are folks the main characters see almost every day, or at least quite frequently. How many of these does the story need? That question can be answered only by the author.

Minor characters are just that; characters who show up occasionally and have a few lines of dialog or walk-ons who don't have any dialog lines.

The size of the cast is dependent on the intricacy of the plot and the number of characters required to get the job done. To solve the plot problem in other words.

For a short story, I think the minimum cast size is three characters; the protagonist, the antagonist and a sidekick for the protagonist.

The presence of a sidekick gives an author an opportunity to present information to the reader using dialog. Without a sidekick, the author can disclose the information through interior monologue. He can also use exposition and simply tell the reader what is going on. The use of a sidekick is the best way of doing this. Using the dialog method also allows the author to throw in some conflict as the two characters argue about the information and how to utilize it.

How many words?

This is a popular question. The popular answer is "As many words as it takes to tell the story." I find this answer factitious. It should also say "unless that many words violate the submission guidelines."

In my opinion, a short story is just that: short. It should be five thousand words or less. Certainly six thousand words is the outer limit. Novels average about eighty thousand words. If you are submitting a short story or a longer work to a publisher, it will have word count guidelines on its website.

So what do you do if your word count exceeds the guidelines? Another reason the answer above is factitious is that it implies the word count necessary to tell the story is an absolute value That is completely false. Stories can be engineered to meet word count guidelines. If the story is too long, there are a number of ways to lower the word count. Eliminate a main character. Eliminate a subplot. Start the story further into the story time.

If you want to increase the word count without simply padding the text with unnecessary words there are other strategies you can employ. Add a main character or subplot or start the story earlier.

In other words, story length is fungible and adaptable.

The "No Rule Rule"

There is another issue to be addressed early on. It's the rule about writing that says, "There are no rules." This is true up to a point. If your name is Stephen King or if you have a few best sellers on your resume, then the Rule applies to you and you can do anything you want and still get published. You can write every other sentences right to left and someone will publish the book.   You can write a book with no punctuation at all and someone will buy and publish it.

If you're just starting out, this Rule doesn't apply to you and I think it's is a terrible thing to tell new writers. Why? Because they may believe it.

Editors do not want to receive submissions from unknown writers who don't follow the rules. Such submissions waste their time. If you don't have a hefty resume filled with prestigious publications and if you're an unknown writer striving for your first publication, believing "The Rule" is a surefire prescription for rapid rejection.

Chapter 2: Setting

Hank Quense: Let's talk about the story's setting. Story setting describes the geography, time and situation in which your story takes place. It also alerts the reader about what to expect from the story.

Author: All right. Bring it on.

HQ: There are two types of setting used in stories. One is the overall story setting, such as Medieval England or a modern, grungy big city. The other type of setting is the kind used in scenes. For instance, a castle keep or dark, rat-infested alley.

Author: Now, you're getting complicated. I don't see the difference.

HQ: Okay. I'll give some examples.

Author: That'll help.

HQ: Suppose you write a story set in your home town. Your story setting would describe the town, its geography, its weather, size and so forth. Individual scenes could be set in the town library, the business district, a park, a private home and a movie theater.

Author: Ahh. That makes sense.

HQ: If the story setting is the Sahara Desert, your story setting would describe the nature of the desert, the change in weather from day to night and other topical information. The story scenes could be set on a sand dune, at an oasis, in an abandoned fortress, in a sand storm. The story setting can also be a house. The various rooms are the setting for scenes.

Author: Okay, I get it.

HQ: We'll talk about scene setting in a subsequent chapter. The setting I'm discussing here refers to the story setting.

Author: Cool. Let's go.

Story setting

Setting can do much more than describe the backdrop for the story. It should convey and define the time period and customs of the characters. It can set up the reader's expectations about the type of story he is about to read. It can start the reader's image-building process.

Consider your characters acting out the story on a stage. Behind the characters, instead of the scenery typical with plays, there is nothing but white panels. The people who paid money to see the play would be dismayed by the lack of scenery, so too your readers will not like it if your story doesn't have the appropriate setting to back up the characters.

As with the plot and other story development elements, the setting must dovetail with the overall story design. As an example, a Medieval setting won't work if the bad guy uses an automatic pistol (unless the bad guy is also a time traveler). Thus the setting places limits on what the author can do and can't do, so it's best if the author has the setting developed before the work gets too far along.

The setting used in your story has to be accurate. Don't try to set a story in Manhattan's Central Park if you haven't been there. Likewise, the French Quarter in New Orleans is unique and shouldn't be used by anyone who hasn't walked the narrow streets.

Here is an example of what can happen. I've lived and worked all my life around New York City. The Hudson River is over a mile wide here and the East River is nearly a half-mile wide. If you haven't been to Dublin, you may assume the Liffey River, which runs through that city, would be of similar size. It isn't. The Liffey is rather small compared to the rivers around Manhattan. Making the Liffey a wide river will destroy your credibility with those readers who have seen the Liffey.

On the other hand, if you develop an imaginary location, you can make the city's river as wide as you want. Similarly, if you use a backdrop of a historical period in the distant past, none of your readers will have been there, but you'll still have to do research to get the setting accurate. You can't use St. Paul's Cathedral with its great dome in London right after William the Conquerer became king of England. St Paul's wasn't built yet.

The setting of the story should be conveyed early to the reader, the earlier the better. Ideally, the opening paragraph in a short story or the first few pages in a longer work should give an indication of the type of story the reader is about to encounter. Is it a mystery set in Victorian London? Is it a story of survival set in war-torn Iraq? Are those vicious aliens on their way to Earth? The reader expects and has a right to know this stuff as early as possible. Don't disappoint the reader. She may put the book down and never open it again.

An effect of establishing the setting is the placing of limitations on the author and the characters. For the author, a space ship means he shouldn't have the characters using swords and landline phones since these artifacts are from bygone eras.

Your characters are also limited. A character in the Old West can't have knowledge of computers or smart phones, unless he's a time-traveler.

If you write a story that uses weapons from a different era or knowledge not available at that time, you'd better have a good reason why it makes sense. You don't have to convince yourself, you have to convince the reader.

Setting Implications

The story setting should be established as soon as possible. There are a number of reasons for this and the most important one is to set up readers' expectations.

The setting also allows a reader to begin building images, a crucial element for reader enjoyment.

For a short story, the setting should be described in the first few paragraphs. For a longer work, the setting can be spread through a few chapters with small bits of setting dropped in at various points. Or, it can be described all at once, provided the exposition isn't so long and detailed that it puts the reader to sleep.

Let's explore how the story setting tells the reader what to expect. Suppose the opening scene or chapter tells the reader a character is leaning against a wall.

In one example, the wall is in a dark alley in Detroit. Rats scurry around foraging for food and the only light comes from a streetlamp at the end of the alley. Suddenly, a second character is illuminated by the light and this character is carrying a machete. Certainly, the reader will expect a dark story, possibly in the horror genre. The reader also suspects a violent event is imminent.

In a second example, the wall the character is leaning against a bulkhead in a spaceship while he looks at a handheld display screen. An alarm sounds and a speaker blares out, "Prepare for collision!" Now the reader understands the story is sci-fi and an emergency is about to unfold.

Lastly, the character is leaning against a wall in the great hall of a castle and three sword-wielding trolls. Now the reader understands she's reading a fantasy adventure story.

If you move the wall into a bedroom and a naked woman enters, the reader expects a completely different type of story.

An important task for the initial setting description is to get the reader to start building images. In the first example, the reader "sees" the dark alley, "hears" the rats and is shocked at the machete. In the second, the reader pictures the handheld screen and listens to the alarm and is jolted by the speaker. The third pictures the swords and the ugly trolls.

Once your reader establishes images in her mind, you've gone a long way to keeping her turning the pages. So, don't upset the reader by pulling a switcheroo on her. Don't dangle one type of story in front of her in the beginning and then change to a completely different type of story.

One last fact about readers. If you don't give them the information they need to build images, they'll build the images without your input. Later on, when you finally give the descriptive information and it contradicts the images the reader has already built, she will be annoyed.

World-building

World-building is an integral part of sci-fi, fantasy and horror stories. Many of these types of stories take place in an imagined setting that exists only in the author's mind.

Sci-fi worlds need to be scientifically accurate in their details. You can't have humans walking on the surface of a gaseous planet as if there is solid ground under their feet. There are web-sites that allow you to build complete solar systems or entire planets including maps. Some sites are free and for some you need a paying account. You can search the web to find an appropriate site. Writer's Digest has at least one article on the subject. You can find a large data base of questions and answers at http://worldbuilding.stackexchange.com

Naturally, the author has to describe the world to the reader, but that is the tricky part of the job. Often the author's ego gets in the way of the reader's enjoyment.

How? Here is an real-life example.

I once critiqued a story for a writer I know. The story took place on an imagined world and concerned a professional player of a complicated game played only on that world. The writer went to great pains to explain — in excruciating detail — how the game was played and how the character used his skill to beat other players. These details consumed several thousand words. During these pages of exposition, the story ground to a standstill. There was no character development and no plot advancement. Just highly technical details that weren't relevant to the story. The reader could have understood and enjoyed the story without knowing about these game details.

This issue addresses another quirk about readers. A reader would have been willing to accept that the game was played on that world and that the character possessed great skill at the game. There was no need to bore the reader with all the details.

In the same story, a visitor to this world took a vehicle to a remote area. Why? So the writer could regale the reader with a detailed description of the world he had imagined. The trip (and the description) had no bearing on the story's plot or its outcome. This description consumed another thousand words of tedious details.

When I pointed out the uselessness of the descriptive passages, the writer disagreed with me and insisted these thousands of words of description were an essential part of the story and couldn't be removed under any conditions.

In a nutshell, the problem here was that the writer was so enthralled with his world-building that he let his ego get in the way of his storytelling.

J.R.R.Tolkien in his *Lord of the Rings* inserts many long world-building passages into the books slowing or stopping the story's forward progress. I've read the series of books a number of times and I have yet to read the world-building passages. And yet, many readers love these passages.

So how does a writer get the important world-building details in front of the reader without boring him to death? This question requires a two-part answer. First, the author has to resist the temptation to write info-dumps, those long wordy passages filled with technical (and boring) details. Second, the author has to decide what details are relevant to the story and /or the characters and drop those details into the story in small bits. This isn't as easy to do as it sounds.

What about the rest of the world-building that doesn't get written into the story? It's background information that allows the author to understand what makes his world tick and why the trains run on time.

In other words, suppress your ego. Great stories aren't about your ego, they are about the story. When given a choice between boring the readers with your creation or telling a great story, choose the great story-telling option every time.

Chapter 3: Characters-1

Hank Quense: Character development is the heart of story design. Going back to the opening definitions, the first key concept mentioned was a character.

Author: Yeah, I remember that. I wasn't too sure what it meant, but I guess you're gonna explain it?

HQ: I am. To develop a well-rounded character you'll have to address four separate areas: physical aspects, mental — or inner — aspects, a character biography and a Dominant Reader Emotion.

Author: What? I thought you just had to tell the reader what the guy looks like. And what's this Dominant thingee? I never heard of that.

HQ: Sorry, you need to address all four areas. In this chapter, I'll talk about the physical aspects and the character's biography. In the next chapter I'll discuss the mental or inner attributes and the Dominant thingee.

Author: Good. You're gonna break it up into small bites

HQ: You have to present the reader with a flesh-and-blood character. You want the reader to develop a mental image for the character, an image that says the character is real to the reader.

Author: That makes sense.

HQ: Yeah, but consider this. Whether the reader's physical image matches your physical image doesn't matter. It's only important that the reader has a physical image that pops up in her mind whenever the character is in a scene. If you think the character resembles your uncle Mortie and the reader thinks the character looks like the guy down the street, the reader's image trumps the author's image.

Author: Really? My character image doesn't count?

HQ: Nope. Only the reader's image counts. Readers take the author's story and make it their own by building images based on the author's words and the reader's life experiences.

Author: Hmm. I guess you're right. If they bought the book, they should get to make their own images.

HQ: Your character doesn't have to be a human, you know?

Author: Yeah, I've seen enough movies about robots and animals to know that.

HQ: But the key point is the non-human character must be endowed with human characteristics. That is, the non-human character must be able to think, to speak and most importantly, to experience emotions.

Author: You mean the robots and animals got to be able to throw a tantrum?

HQ: Right. Let's wrap this up with a few more words about the differences between physical and mental attributes.

Author: Okay.

HQ: The physical aspects of a character are what the five senses can observe. For the readers, sight and hearing are the two primary senses, but smell and touch also apply. Taste is a tricky one. Why would a reader want to know what a character tastes like? Well, the story could have sex scenes in it. Or maybe the story is about cannibals.

Author: Yuck!

HQ: The mental aspects of a character for the most part can't be "seen" by the reader, but they are more much important facets of the character's make up. Let's move on.

Physical features

To begin with, the physical features can be divided into three areas: appearance, traits and speaking.

The physical appearance is straightforward and there is nothing tricky about it. Under this heading you need to provide information on the color of the character's skin, hair and eyes. Height, weight and build are also necessary. Clothing falls into this category also, but this has to be realistic. You can't have a character wearing a ski jacket at the beach in the middle of summer, unless there is a reason for this bizarre development.

Traits can be difficult to develop and require a bit of creativity to ensure all the characters in the story are different. These traits fall into the following categories: tics, movement, speech and features like a scar. These are also called individualization traits.

Tics: Tics are habits, usually unconscious ones, that set the character apart from other characters in the story. An example is a woman who curls a hank of hair whenever she is thinking. After mentioning this a few times, you won't have to tell the reader she's thinking; you just have to "show" her curling her hair. Another tic can have the character pulling a face whenever someone disagrees with him.

Movement: The way a character moves can be good way of differentiating him from other characters. Your character can walk with a limp or use a cane. Other movement options are walking faster or slower than others.

Speech: Does your character talk with a lisp? Does she stutter? Does she pepper her speech with foreign words? These bits of development can be used to make a character different from others.

Scars: A facial scar is a defining trait. So is a tattoo. Birthmarks or skin discoloration also fall into this category.

If you decide your character limps, or has a scar, make sure your biographical material covers what happened to the character. How did the character get the limp or scar?

If you commute to work on a bus or a train, you have a great opportunity to observe fellow commuters and pick up some of these physical aspects.

I use a character form to hold all the information on each character in a story. Part of the form is reproduced below. This portion concerns the physical aspects only. Story function or role is what the character's job is in the story. Typical jobs are protagonist, antagonist, sidekick, major character, subplot protagonist (or antagonist), minor character etc. Depending on the story design, a character can play more than one role. For instance, the protagonist's sidekick can also be the protagonist in one or more subplots.

The categories in the form are straightforward. Copy these into a word processor and build your own character form.

Character Description Form

Character Name:
Story Function:
Physical Traits:
Biographical Material:
Dress Habits:
Dialog:

As you build the characters, you may notice that limitations crop up. A character can't do what you want him to do because he is too old. An elderly person, for instance, can't do many things a younger person can do.
You are becoming limited in what you, the author, can do and what your characters can do or can not do. These limitations or restrictions will also occur with plotting and motivation. The more the story design develops, the less freedom you and your characters have. As an example, if you build a character's physical aspects so that he has a serious limp, you can't have him outrunning the bad guy. Similarly, if your character dropped out of high school, he can't use the laws of thermodynamics to develop the solution to the plot problem. This is one huge advantage to building a complete biography; it gives you a better understanding of what the character is capable of doing.

Biography

A biography for the character serves a dual purpose. Besides providing background information, it allows the author to understand the character and that understanding is vital when dealing with the character in stressful situations.

For a short-story character, I write a few paragraphs of bio material. For the main character in a novel, the bio may run to more than a page. Other novel characters will get less of a bio. The less important the character, the smaller the bio I create.

The strange thing to many new story writers is this: most of the biographical material won't show up in the story so why bother developing it? The answer is that the bio allows the writer to understand the character and what makes him or her tick. The better the writer knows and understands the character, the better the writer will be able to predict how the character will respond to situations and stimuli.

For instance, suppose someone walks up to your character and punches him in the mouth, or a beautiful woman kisses him. How does your character react to the punch? Does he punch back? Does he walk away? How does the character react to the kiss? Does he get red in the face? Does he kiss her back? Does he develop a stammer? Your detailed biography will guide you in writing the character's response. If you don't have the bio material, the character's response is really a guess. In addition, the writer will have difficulty keeping the character's response consistent when other situations occur. Your second guess may be different from your first guess. Believe me, the readers will pick up on it.

There are a number of biographical elements the writer should address.

Family: Are his parents alive? Does the character have any siblings? What is everyone's age? Are any siblings married? Where did the character grow up? Did the character have any unusual childhood experiences? What were they? Do these experiences affect the character? Is the character's family stable? Or is it chaotic? How does this affect him?

Education: Schools, degrees, favorite subject?

Career: Jobs, military experience?

Adult experiences: Married? Divorced? Children?

It's the author's job to come up with events that will affect the character's life and outlook.

Dialog

I believe that dialog is the most important aspect of the physical characteristics.

Dialog could have been discussed under Storytelling Techniques, but I choose to cover it under character building.

I'm sure you understand that characters can't all look alike. All your men can't be hunks and all your female characters can't be green-eyed and red-haired with voluptuous figures.

What you may not understand is that they all can't speak the same. If all the characters speak with the same style, the same emotional level, and use the same words, your dialog will be boring and sound stilted. Your readers will notice the lack of differences and will not be amused — or entertained and they will likely get confused about who is speaking.

Each main character should have a unique way of speaking. At a minimum, there must be something to differentiate each character's dialog from the other characters' manner of speaking. Minor characters and walk-ons don't need a special way of talking.

Does one of your characters drop the -g in -ing words: i.e. sayin', goin', leavin' and so forth? Does your character use words such as gonna, wanna, outta, inna?   Both of these usages will give your characters a bit of individuality in their dialog as long as every character doesn't speak this way.

Some characters use short direct sentences, others are long-winded and use many words to say"no."

Part of an individual's dialog habits will depend upon how you built your character. A banker for instance, will tend to speak in financial terms. A street punk will use slang and street talk and will definitely not talk like the banker. A college professor will lean toward using big or unusual words while a truck driver will not. Don't have your truck driver sounding like a physics professor. If your character grew up in France (consult your bio for the character to find out) you can differentiate his dialog by slipping in a few French words. "Hello, *mon ami*." or "*Bonjour*, Kathy." The danger here is overdoing it with the French words. Even worse, having the character mistakenly use Italian or Spanish words instead of French. Make sure you know what the character is saying.

Dialog should also reflect the character's emotional state. If two characters are having a furious argument, their dialog must reflect that state. They can't be speaking as if they're discussing last night's ballgame. Their dialog has to have in-your-face elements to it. If your character is in a vexing situation that demands an important decision, his dialog should reflect a degree of hesitation as the character stalls to gain time to think about the decision.

As you can see, writing dialog isn't all easy or simple.

Conversation

Inexperienced writers often confuse dialog with conversation. These are not the same things. Dialog moves the story along; conversation stops the story in its tracks.

So, how do you tell the difference? If the character's words either characterize someone or move the plot forward, it's dialog. If the speech does neither, it's conversation.

Consider this snippet of talk between two characters:

"Hey, dude," Tom said. "How's it going?"

"I'm cool," Joe replied. "Gonna watch the Yankee game tonight?"

"Wouldn't miss it. I love to watch Yankees beat up on Boston."

"Me, too." Joe grinned at the thought of a Yankee win. "Hey! Wanna go to the bar to watch the game? We can suck up a few brews."

"Good idea," Tom replied. "I'll meet you there around seven o'clock."

"Cool," Joe said. "See you there."

Is this dialog or conversation? It depends upon the situation and the plot. Will the Yankee game become an event in the story's plot? Will something important happen during the game? Will something dramatic happen in the bar that evening? Does being Yankee fans somehow characterize Joe or Tom?

If the answer to all these questions is "No," then this is conversation and it should be deleted since its only purpose is to slow down the story and add to the word count.

However, if Joe gets shot by the antagonist while in the bar that night, then this is dialog since the sequence leads Joe to be at a place where he will get shot.

While the distinction is murky at times, you can use this test to decide if the talk is conversation or dialog. Remove it from the scene. Did anything change about the scene or the story's plot? If the answer is no, then nothing will change if it's removed because it's conversation, not dialog and therefore unnecessary.

Chapter 4: Characters-2

Hank Quense: Memorize the following: Memorable stories have memorable characters! Memorable characters are ones with the complex inner workings.

Author: That's pretty deep.

HQ: There's more. No character ever became memorable on his physical aspects alone.

Author: Why do I think you're about to get into some heavy-duty stuff?

HQ: You're correct. Try this on for size. Many new writers assume that once they have developed the physical aspects of the character, they are finished with the character development. What these writers have built is a cardboard cutout of a real character.

Author: I knew it. Now you're telling me that the physical stuff I did isn't any good.

HQ: What you did is important, but there are more significant attributes to go over in this chapter. That's what we'll be working on.

Author: Uh-oh.

HQ: The important thing to remember about the inner workings of a character is that these are the qualities that turn the cardboard character into a "real" character, one that is 'human.' The mental aspects of character development are crucially important. It's a question of building a character the reader will like to spend time with or one that will bore the reader. This is where you should spend the bulk of your time.

Author: Ahh, maybe this won't be so bad.

HQ: Every real-life person is a unique individual. The same applies to your characters. Your characters can't all look alike; they all can't speak the same and they can't all think alike. You'll have to use your creativity to build unique characters.

Mental aspects

Nothing tells the reader the author is an amateur quicker than reading about a make-believe cardboard character, one that isn't a "real" person. As you develop this part of your character you will, once again, run into the limitation factor. The more defined your character becomes, the more limitations you'll place on the character and yourself.

In this section we'll cover the mental or inner workings of characters. There are a number of areas involved in this undertaking and it will require creativity and hard work to finish the development. These areas include the character's personality, his dreams, his aspirations and mirages that affect him. The character's philosophy is also an important element here and that will be covered separately.

Personality: Let's start with personality. Here is a definition from the American Heritage Dictionary: *The pattern of feelings, thoughts, and activities that distinguishes one person from another*. If you scan the web, you'll find a bewildering array of web sites about personality including some heavy-duty stuff from doctors. Basically, it seems to break down into two areas: personality types and personality traits.

According to one theory, there are sixteen types of personality. There are four types in each of four categories: analysts, diplomats, sentinels and explorers. Your character has to be one of sixteen. For more information see http://www.16personalities.com/personality-types.

Within these categories, there are many personality traits. You need to define your character by giving him or her a personality trait or two. Is your character affable, charming, pompous, unfriendly? There are many personality traits that can be used. Once you select one or two, do a web search on that trait to ensure you can write convincingly about that type of personality. There is more information about personality traits here: http://examples.yourdictionary.com/examples-of-personality-traits.html

Dreams (aspirations): What does your character want out of life? What does he want to do when he grows up? What does she want to achieve? This attribute can influence how the character acts and can provide a measure of conflict. What if she wants to become an engineer, but has to decide whether to stay in college or drop out to help her sick mother? This situation will provide inner conflict.

Memories: These are influencers that characters have. Memories can also be used for foreshadowing and to build up internal conflict. How? Consider this example: as a five-year-old, the character almost drowned. Ever since, she has had a healthy fear of open water. At some point in the story, she sees a man drowning in the middle of a lake. What does your character do? Does her fear of water cause her to ignore the man and walk away? Does she search for a boat to use in the rescue? Does she suppress her fear and dive into the lake?

This inner conflict can provide a memorable scene in the story. Remember though, a heroine has to do heroic stuff. It would be acceptable for a villainess to let the guy drown, but a heroine will have to try to save him, or she won't be believable. If she lets the guy drown without trying to save him, the character will be seen as a phony and the reader will lose interest in her.

Another example will concern a man who was punished as a child by being locked in a dark closet. Now he fears dark basements, caves, alleys and any unlit place. You can see how this memory and foreshadowing can lead to exciting scenes and gripping internal conflict.

Mirages: These are fantasies the character tricks herself into believing. Want an example? Most politicians thinking they have the slightest chance of getting elected President.

Descriptor (or voice): This item isn't the same as the way the character speaks, it's a brief description or summary of the character and the way he thinks and acts. This isn't easy to develop but I believe it's essential to have one for the major and main characters. Once you have the descriptor, it will help you write accurately about the character and his thoughts, his actions, his reactions.

Examples may be the best way to explain the descriptor. A banker can be the voice of greed and will endlessly talk about money and financial concerns. This character will always be trying to get more money, possibly through fraud. A psychopath is the voice of rage, always ready for an argument or fight. A warrior could be described as the voice of chaos. An accountant can be the voice of precision.

Philosophy

Everyone has a personal philosophy. You have one whether you realize it or not, whether you want one or not. I don't know if a personal philosophy comes with your birth package or is a product of your environment and your upbringing. To me, how it happened isn't as important as recognizing that it did happen. My personal philosophy is skepticism with a healthy dose of cynicism. Since all people have a personal philosophy, it follows that your main and major characters should also have a personal philosophy.

Assign a philosophy to a character and instantly, limitations follow. For instance, if your character's philosophy is individualism, you can't have him acting hesitant or asking other characters for help and answers. An individualist character tends to do stuff by himself. He's decisive, not wishy-washy. Similarly, if the character is an optimist, you can't have her bad-mouthing everybody's ideas and suggestions. That's the way a pessimist will act.

Here is a list of philosophies I use for my characters and the definition of each.

Animism: Belief in conscious life, or soul, of inanimate objects as well as living beings.

Empiricism: A view that sense perception and experience are sole foundations of knowledge.

Fatalism: All events and occurrences are predetermined and inevitable.

Hard-Determinism: There is no free will nor non-predetermined action.

Hedonism: A doctrine of pleasure as the highest or only good.

Hylozoism: Life is inherent in all matter whether animal, vegetable or mineral.

Individualism: Philosophical theory emphasizing personal freedom and autonomy.

Materialism: Reality consists solely of matter without separate reality of mind or spirit.

Idealism: Theory that reality is a creation of mind, and that mental and spiritual values, rather than matter, constitute reality; immaterialism.

Mysticism: Doctrine of direct inexplicable knowledge and experience of truth and reality without rational processes or reliance on creed, orthodoxy or belief systems.

Naturalism: Theory that reality consists solely of the natural, observable world with no supernatural or spiritual realm.

Nihilism: Social and economic order is inherently corrupt and morality cannot be justified.

Optimism: Doctrine holding that reality is fundamentally good and the world is governed by benign forces.

Pessimism: Reality is fundamentally evil and the world is governed by malevolent forces.

Perspectivism: Reality and truth are known only from the perspective of the individual or group viewing them at a particular moment.

Pragmatism: Emphasizes consequences and practical results of one's conduct rather than principles and categories of reality.

Skepticism: Theory that man can never attain certain knowledge and that all knowledge should be questioned.

There are other philosophies that can be used, but this list has almost all the ones you need. Anything not on this list will be a pretty weird philosophy and it will be difficult to get readers to buy into it.

Dominant Reader Emotion

This isn't part of the character's inner or outer aspects. It also isn't part of the character's biography. The Dominant Reader's Emotion (DRE) is the emotion you want (hope!) the reader will experience whenever the character is in a scene. There are a number of reader emotions you can use. Typical emotions are: admiration, sympathy, pity, dislike, annoyance and many more.

Whatever reader emotion you choose dictates the way you write about the character and limits what you can have the character do. For example, if you wish the reader to like a character, you can't have that character kicking puppies or pushing little old ladies in front of buses. You can have a character do these things if the reader emotion you're striving for is anger or disgust.

In creating a new character, I assign a DRE early on because it affects the development process for that character. If I want a character to be sympathetic to a reader, I can't create a willful, powerful, egotistical character because it will be difficult for a reader to be sympathetic to such an unrealistic character. The reader probably has never met such a person and if she has met such a person, it probably wasn't a comfortable experience.

A difficult feat (but not an impossible one) is to have the reader start off with one dominant emotion about a main character and have that reader's emotion gradually change over the course of the story. This is not possible to carry out in a short story because it is too short to make such a change without confusing the reader. However, in a novel, script or memoir there is room for the character to learn and grow substantially. This maturation can lead to a gradual change from one dominant emotion to a different one.

In my novel *Moxie's Problem* the title character starts off as an obnoxious, whiny, teenage princess. The DRE here is annoyance. Over the course of the novel, Moxie realizes her situation, puts together a plan to change her life and begins to implement the plan. During the story, the DRE changes to sympathy. In the conclusion to Moxie's story *Moxie's Decision* — a second novel — Moxie continues to grow into a decisive, strong woman and the reader's DRE continues to change and becomes admiration.

This type of character growth or change makes for a story that readers love.

Here is a list of Dominant Reader Emotions that I use in my stories.

Affection: The reader develops a fondness or liking for the character.

Anger: The reader feels displeasure with the character.

Animosity: The character arouses anger in the reader.

Delight: The reader takes pleasure in the character and his/her actions.

Disgust: The reader is revolted by the character

Empathy: The reader relates to the character and thinks the character is just like the reader; i.e. the character and the reader share common traits.

Hostility: The reader is decidedly unfriendly toward the character.

Irritation: The reader is annoyed by the character.

Pity: The reader feels sorry for the character.

Sympathy: The reader understands the character. Note that this is very different from empathy despite the similarity in spelling.

Sadness: The reader feels sorry or unhappy for the character

There are many more emotions that can be used besides these. Finding them will be your homework assignment.

Character Development Sheet

Below is another part of my character development sheet. Some items will be described in following sections.

Philosophy
Dominant Reader Emotion
Descriptor (voice)
Personality
Type
Positive traits
Negative traits
Character Arc
Motivation
Dreams (Aspirations)
Memories that influence the motivation
Mirages that a character fools himself into believing

Put these categories into the sheet with the physical aspects and you'll have your own character template.

Chapter 5: More Character Stuff

Hank Quense: This brief chapter covers additional topics pertaining to characters, but which aren't directly related to the character development process.

Author: What's that supposed to mean? Sounds like double talk.

HQ: I'm about to discuss character arc, motivation, villain types and mind-maps.

Author: Mind-maps? You're kidding, right?

HQ: I'm not kidding. All of these topics are important.

Author: I'll stick around for a while, but I'm getting ready to run.

HQ: Hey! Learning to create stories isn't easy. There's a lot of stuff you won't want to hear, but I'm telling you anyway.

Character Arc

Every story needs a character arc. This topic isn't really part of the character development, it's more related to the plot, but it's the result of the plot rather than part of the plot. That sounds confusing doesn't it?

Basically, there are two types of character arcs. One concerns itself with what great lesson the main character(s) learn over the course of the story. The second is what changes in the life of the character(s) as a result of the events in the story.

The character arc applies to the antagonist as well as the protagonist. That assumes the bad guy is still alive after the story ends. If the antagonist is dead, well, maybe he did learn something, but it was a bit too late to be useful.

If there is no character arc then everything after the story ends is the same as before the story began. Nothing happened, in other words. The only thing that changed is that the characters got older. A story without a character arc is an incomplete and unsatisfactory story.

The character arc can be physical or mental or both, but a mental character arc is more interesting than a physical one. In a mental character arc, the character learned an important lesson. In a physical one, the character's situation changed for better or worse.

To get a deeper understanding for character arcs, we can look at a few examples.

A character starts out as a bigot, but during the course of the story, learns to be less bigoted and becomes more open-minded.

Another example concerns itself with a proud or pompous (or both) character who gets humbled as the story unfolds.

A lazy character gets motivated.

A character evolves from an uninterested bystander or a follower into the leader of a movement.

Here are examples of a great character arc from the movies.

In Star Wars, Luke Skywalker evolves from a rustic farm boy into a Jedi knight (and it only took three movies for that to happen).

In Lord of the Rings, both the books and the movies, Frodo evolves. As a result of his journey, he changes from an inexperienced youth to a strong-minded, decisive man (or hobbit, to be more precise).

Antagonist development

Naturally, writers spend a great deal of time developing the protagonist for their stories. After all, this character is the star of the story. But for the protagonist to really shine, he has to contend with a well-developed antagonist. In a nutshell, that means the writer has to spend time developing a bad guy who is as interesting as the good guy.

It may come as a surprise to some that the bad guy doesn't have to be 'bad.' The antagonist can be just as moral, dedicated and upright as the good guy. Nevertheless, the antagonist has to strive to defeat the protagonist or to keep the good guy from succeeding.

Here is an example to explain this conundrum. Suppose the world is threatened by pollution or an alien invasion. Both character A (the protagonist) and character B (the antagonist) develop plans to save the world. A thinks B's plan is terrible and will only serve to increase the danger. B thinks the same thing about A's plan. So the conflict here is between and A and B as they strive to have their plans accepted and implemented. Notice that both have the same goal: to save the world. Their only difference concerns how to go about saving the world.

To be sure, many antagonists are not nice guys. There are a number of types of villainy possible. You should select one and develop the antagonist accordingly.

Here is a list of villain types. This is based on the ebook *Writing About Villains* by Rayne Hall.

The Evil Overlord is at the top of a power pyramid and wants still more power.

The Schemer fits into any society. Plans for the long term.

The Obsessed Scientist is intelligent, analytical, creative and determined.

The Smothering Mother dominates her family or community or club.

The Fanatic is motivated by deeply held, often religious convictions.

The Seductress uses her charms (either her mind or body) to get what she wants.

The Sadist's motivation is pleasure at victims pain or fear.

The Confidence Trickster is good at reading people, adaptable, confident, persuasive, inspiring.

The Social Reject stands outside society. He may be an outlaw, a nerd or misfit.

The Bully is picks on vulnerable victims, motivated by the short-term power boost his ego gets.

Once you assign the villain type, make sure your character development supports that type of villain.

Motivation

Think about your protagonist. He has to solve a plot problem. That's the character's job. Your character has to get up off the couch, go out into the cruel world and possibly risk his life in order to solve the problem.

Why should he go through all this effort? That's the question you, the author, have to answer. What's the character's motivation? Why does he feel he has to solve the problem? Why doesn't he say, "Let someone else do it." Or, "I'm too busy." Or, "Maybe I'll do it later."

The lack of proper motivation is a death knell for a story. The reader will never buy into a story in which the protagonist has a half-hearted motive. Not only does the character have to be truly motivated, the author has to convince the reader that the character's motivation is real; that the character truly believes he has to solve the plot problem. The more serious the plot problem is, the stronger the motivation has to be. You can't have a dilatory effort to track down a serial killer. Nor can you have an all-out effort by the entire cast to find a Mother's Day card. If the characters are risking their lives, the motivation has to reflect the seriousness of the situation.

Simply put, motivation is what drives the protagonist to solve the plot problem and it's what drives the antagonist to struggle to prevent the good guy from succeeding. Both the protagonist and the antagonist have to be motivated and these two motivations have to be commensurate in strength. You can't have a highly motivated protagonist facing off against an antagonist who is only mildly motivated.

To complicate the motivation problem, the motivation has to be consistent with the character's persona. A meek, mild-mannered character can't suddenly start acting like a combat-experienced mercenary.

Motivation is another area where what you can do and what the character can do is limited by the character you built. Motivation has to be in sync with the DRE, the philosophy and the bio you gave the character. If all these elements don't match each other, the character's actions will not be believable, because his actions from scene to scene will not be consistent.

Inner and outer motivation: A complex character, the kind readers love, should have both outer and inner motivation. The outer motive is fairly easy to develop. It is usually based on solving the plot problem. Once this problem is resolved, the outer motive has been met. The inner motive is more complicated. It can be almost anything and doesn't have to be related to the plot problem. The best combination of motives is a pair of mutually exclusive ones; the protagonist can't achieve one without giving up the other. This constraint sets up natural internal conflict in the character and can lead to unexpected plot twists that will keep the reader involved. Effectively, the author has constructed an engine of motivation and anti-motivation.

As an example of conflicting inner and outer motives, consider this situation: the protagonist has to rescue a man trapped on a mountain. He does this because it's his job. That's the protag's outer motive. But the rescued man is engaged to the woman the protag loves. That is the protag's inner motive; to romance the woman of his dreams whom he'll lose if he succeeds with his outer motive. It is easy to see the great internal conflict that will harass this protagonist. Should he let the guy die and then try to marry the woman? Should he rescue the guy and lose the woman?

This combination of competing inner and outer motives can draw readers into the story and hold them. Will the character murder for love or selflessly lose the woman? Whatever he does, it must be consistent with his persona. If he is narcissistic, he may choose murder. If he is law-abiding, he may elect to save the guy. Whatever he chooses to do, his motivation must be made clear to the reader.

Antagonist's motivation: Successful stories need conflict, tension and emotions from more than just the protagonist. If a properly motivated protagonist strives to solve the plot problem and doesn't encounter an equally motivated antagonist, the story will lack the conflict that produces the tension that leads to emotional outbursts. Hence, the author must develop strong motives for the bad guy to keep the struggle equal. The stronger the bad guy's motives, the stronger the story will be.

Lack of a reason or motivation: Quite often the reason a character does something or the motivation that drives a response is lost to the reader. This confusion occurs because the author has neglected to include the character's motivation in the scene or the snippet of action. A snippet is a short piece of action embedded into scenes. It contains a stimulus sentence or two followed by a character's response. This sequence of action is also called cause and effect. Unfortunately, the two elements are frequently reversed or left incomplete to the confusion of the reader.

Sometimes the motivation is apparent, such as when a character jumps behind a wall when he hears a shot. In this case, the reader doesn't have to have the motivation explained to her. When a reaction isn't that apparent, it is essential that the author describe the character's motivation or stimulus. In the following snippet of a scene, Jody is a minor character about whom the reader knows nothing:

Danny worked on the old car and whistled a nameless tune.
"Hi, Danny," Jody said, giving him a big smile.
"Shut up or I'll make you shut up," Danny snarled.
Jody turned on her heel and left.

In this example, the reader is left clueless why Danny snarled at Jody.

Many times when this problem surfaces, it has to do with a character reacting angrily, even violently, for no apparent reason. It's as if the author understands the need for tension or conflict, but inserts it randomly into the story without defining the character's motivation. This artificial tension will come across as contrived and will be counterproductive. This type of motivation-less action occurs more often than you'd think possible and turns reading a story from an enjoyable pastime into a chore.

A common example of the lack of motivation occurs when the author writes "character X grinned," or "character X chortled," and the author neglects to tell the reader why the character grinned or chortled. If you're reading along and suddenly stop to wonder, "What just happened?" you've probably found a place where the author omitted the character's motivation. More about this in Chapter 10.

Mind-maps

In a short story, keeping the characters' attributes straight usually isn't a large problem because of the limited cast of characters. In a longer work, the attributes can present a problem to the author. The cast of characters in a novel can easily be a dozen or more main and major characters. So how do you keep track of the most important attributes? Do you print the character sheets and thumb through them every time a character shows up in a scene? How do you remember what the DRE is for each character? Getting these attributes wrong or inconsistent will lead to a baffled reader.

The important attributes that affect the scene writing are role, DRE, voice, philosophy and descriptor. You can build a table to list this material, but I like to see information displayed graphically so I use mind-maps to show this information.

I'm not going to explain mind-maps here. If you know about them, there is a good chance you use them and will understand this section. If you aren't familiar with mind-maps, many web-sites have good explanations on how to use and develop mind-maps. Mind-map usage is explained in more detail in Chapter 15.

The first step in making a character mind-map is to make a template to copy and reuse. Below is a copy of the character template I use.

Once the template is finished, I copy it and paste it into a mind-map program as many times as I need (based on how many characters I need). After that, I fill in the relevant data and print it.

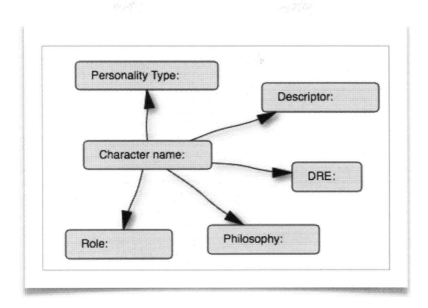

This template obviously doesn't contain nearly as much information as the full character sheet, but it does have the necessary information for me to write scenes without looking up the character sheets. Think of this as a cheat sheet to simplify my job of writing scenes. I print the mind-map and keep the copy handy while I'm writing.

The template shown here was created in Junkyard, a Mac mind-map program. I have a number of mind-mapping programs but Junkyard is one I use frequently.

Here is the completed template for a single character. This is the title character for Moxie's Problem and Moxie's Decision.

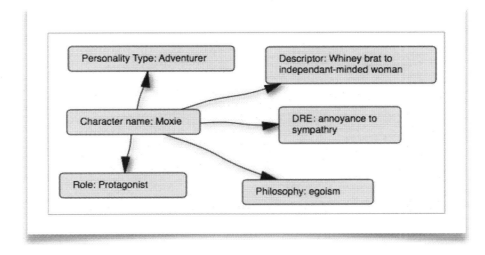

Notice Moxie's DRE and the Descriptor show a change over the course of the story. While this single character mind-map is instructive, you'll have to picture how valuable it would be with a dozen characters on a single mind-map.

Granted this takes time to do and requires a software program. However, I think the time spent is worth it. Consider this. Writing a novel involves a lot of work and consumes a lot of time. An important issue is character consistency. Each appearance by a character has to look and feel to the reader the same as the last appearance. This consistency is difficult to achieve without some method of rapidly retrieving relevant information about the character. That is what this mind-map does. It allows me to quickly scan the major character data.

Part 2:Plotting

Chapter 6: Plotting

Hank Quense: So, you have a bunch of characters ready to rumble. Right now the cast of characters is unemployed.

Author: Say what?   What does that mean?

HQ: It means the characters don't have a job.

Author: But what if they have a plot problem to work on?

HQ: The plot problem is a job offer, not a job. They won't have a job until you develop a plot.

Author: Huh?

HQ: The plot tells the characters what to do. It's a list of events and tasks to solve the plot problem and, after all, solving the plot problem is the Good Guy's job. Opposing the Good Guy is the Bad Guy's job.

Author: Whoa! That's a different way to explain it.

HQ: Here's another explanation. Think of a stage with actors standing around. The actors aren't doing anything because the director hasn't told the actors what to do. Your plot is the story's director. It tells the characters how to solve the plot problem. So, without the plot, the characters are just hanging out, waiting.

Author: All right. I'm convinced. I gotta get these bums working. Wait? How do I do that?

HQ: I thought you'd never ask.

Developing a plot requires a lot of creativity and thinking. You may not be able to complete it right away. I have story ideas from years ago that I haven't been able to construct a plot for. The sticking point is this: The plot you build must be one that YOU believe in. If you don't, you'll never be able to convince the reader to believe in it.

Now that I've introduced the concept of mind-maps in the previous chapter, I'll use them to explain concepts. A picture really does save a lot of words.

Here is a mind-map providing an overview of the plot concerns.

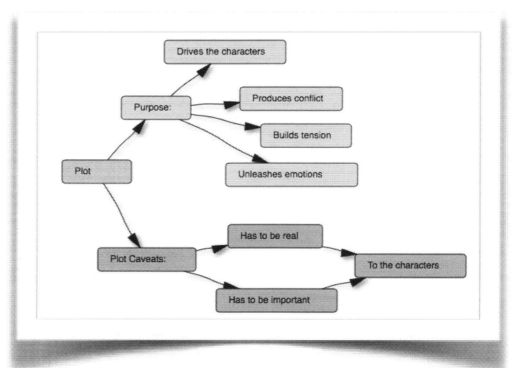

Study the graphic. You can see the plot has a four-part purpose and the plot problem has two caveats.

Plot purpose:

Drives the characters: we just discussed this in the previous section: the plot gives the characters a job and tells them how to go about doing the job. The plot moves the characters forward.

Provides conflict: Besides driving the characters to solve the plot problem, it also provides conflict. The conflict doesn't have to be limited to the protagonist versus the antagonist. The conflict should be expanded to involve more characters. The more conflicts going on, the better. For example, suppose both the protagonist and the antagonist have sidekicks who are major characters in the story. The guys on the good team can yell and shout and argue about the best way to solve the plot problem. The bad team, meanwhile, can argue the reverse, how to prevent the plot problem from getting solved. All this arguing and disagreement is entertaining to the reader

Builds tension: All this conflict isn't merely for the reader to enjoy. The conflict builds tension among the characters. For instance, the hero and his friend are getting stressed out by their constant bickering over how to approach the plot problem. This tension can affect the reader and have her biting her nails anticipating the next furious argument. The reader can also worry that the bickering can derail the character's efforts or distract the characters and make it harder for them to solve the plot problem.

Emotions: The more conflict there is and the more serious the situation becomes, the stronger the characters' emotions have to be. You can't have a protagonist fail a few times and have a lackluster emotional response. "Oh well, what the hell. I'll get it right the next time," is not a good emotional response to failure. The emotional level has to reflect the characters' failures (or successes in the case of the antagonist).

As the reader gets deeper into the story, he'll experience ever-growing emotional trauma in the characters and that's good. Readers read stories to experience these emotional journeys.

Subplots are a good way to extend the tension and conflict and to stretch out the reader's emotional journey and her anticipation. More about subplots in the next chapter.

Plot caveats:

Has to be real: The plot problem is the reason for the story. Consequently, it has to be a real problem the characters deal with. Both the protagonist and the antagonist have to be convinced this problem is real and serious. If the protagonist is serious about the plot problem and the antagonist treats it as a minor concern, the conflict will be unbalanced. That lack of equality in the response will jolt the reader to stop reading.

Has to be important: The reader can think the plot problem is silly or not very serious. That's all right, provided the author convinces the reader that the characters believe the problem is real (to the characters) and serious (to the characters).

Plot Path

The plot of a story is the path the author uses to navigate the almost endless possible alternatives between the story's opening and its conclusion.

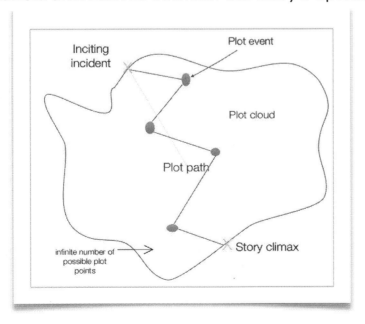

The plot is a sequence of important events, a path in other words. Important in this case means that the events have serious consequences for the characters. The story starts with the Inciting incident. This is the event that triggers the hero's reaction and marks the beginning of his search for a solution. Construction of this plot path is the most difficult part of the story development. The plot path consists of a series of events that will take the reader on a journey from the inciting incident to the climax of the story. To illustrate this sequence, I use a device called the plot cloud shown above. The inciting incident is also called the inciting event.

The plot cloud contains every conceivable event that could be used in your plot. There are an infinite number of them inside the cloud. Your job is to find the small number of plot events that will allow you to construct the plot path. Once you string those events together, you have a plot path. Unfortunately, since there are an infinite number of plot events, there are also an infinite number of potential plot paths through the cloud. Now, that's a scary thought, isn't it. That's what makes plot construction so hard.

Most of the possible plot paths are ludicrous or just silly and have to be discarded. The author's job is to find those events that will make his story believable. If the author develops a plot path that he doesn't really believe in, the path must be discarded and the author has to start all over again. Why? Because the author has to believe in the plot or he'll never convince the reader to believe in it.

Constructing a plot

To repeat, a plot consists of a series of events that connect the inciting incident to the story's climax.

Events are not the same as incidents in this context. What's the difference? Events are major happenings or plot twists. Incidents are everyday occurrences. Humdrum and ordinary, they are the stuff that should be omitted from the story for the most part. For instance, let's suppose a character wakes up in the morning. If you then describe her routine of taking a shower, putting on makeup, selecting an outfit to wear to work and eating breakfast, these are all incidents. You, the author, have to ask yourself why am I even writing about this stuff? All it does is slow down the story, consume words and bore the readers.

However, if the woman's estranged husband replaced the water in the water heater with sulphuric acid, then the shower becomes an event: a very messy one.

Constructing a plot is a three-step process. The first step is to come up with a plot problem for the characters to work on. The second step is to develop the story's ending. The third step is to develop a series of events to connect step one and step two. After that, you are ready to write the first draft, provided all the other design work has been completed.

That's all there is to it, but don't be deceived by this simple formula. It's hard work.

Step two may be a shock to some. It may seem counterintuitive at first, but it isn't. The purpose of a story is to take the reader on a journey from the beginning to the story's climax. Everything in the story must take the reader closer and closer to the climax. If you're writing a first draft and you haven't figured out the ending yet, how can you move the reader closer to the climax? The story's climax doesn't exist yet.

Let's develop a generic plot path for a story.

      One: Hero recognizes the plot problem.

      Two: Hero makes an effort to solve the plot problem and fails.

      Three: A second and more serious effort also fails.

      Four: A third desperate attempt ends in a disaster.

      Five: A do-or-die attempt follows.

      Six: The hero succeeds (or not).

In a short story, these steps could become the scenes in the story. In a longer work, each step could be several chapters.

What's the point of all these successive failures? To jerk the reader around emotionally. As the protagonist repeatedly fails, the tension increases and the characters' emotions become stronger. The tension and the emotions affect the readers and keep them turning the pages.

After step six, you need one more scene: the validation scene. This scene describes what the reward is for all the hero's hard work. Does he win the gold medal? Does he get a big kiss from a beautiful woman? Does he find the treasure? The validation scene is the final scene in the story. In a longer work, the validation scene can become the validation chapter as you wrap up all the loose ends.

All these factors contribute to a key element in the story construction: the story's emotional arcs.

Emotional arcs

Once the plot is built, you can then work on developing the emotional arcs. These arcs are the most powerful way to keep readers engrossed in the story. An emotional arc tracks the emotional changes the main characters undergo during the course of the story.

For the protagonist, the arc is downward as the failures pile up. For the antagonist, the arc moves upward since the good guy's failures are the bad guy's successes. A story in which the main characters' emotional changes are flat or stagnant is a poorly design story and one that will not hold a reader's interest. In other words, a flat emotional arc is a bummer.

At the climax of the story, the protagonist's emotional state is as low as it can go while the antagonist's is as high as it can be. The good guy despairs from his failures while the bad guy is giddy with success. During the climax, these emotional extremes will undergo severe changes.

How do you construct these emotional arcs? They're a byproduct of scene design combined with plotting and will be discussed in Chapter 8. It's sufficient for now that you understand the concept of and the need for the emotional arcs.

Conflict

One of the main purposes of a plot is to generate conflict within the cast of characters. While the conflict can be between two characters, a three-sided battle provides more opportunities for conflicts. This three-sided combat also leads to the concept of a conflict triangle. Each of the three characters is now striving against two opponents. This type of conflict is depicted below. Character A and Character B can represent the protagonist and antagonist. Character C can be a sidekick or even a third main character who tries to outwit both A and B.

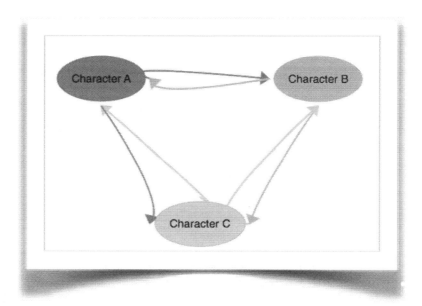

This is a very powerful technique to increase the conflict and the resultant tension in a story. Over the course of the story, the architecture of the triangle can change.   An example of this can happen if Character B becomes an ally of Character A against Character C. The conflict triangle now looks like this.

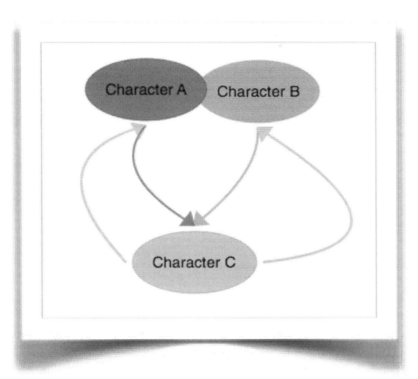

Another technique to complicate the situation is to have Character B switch sides a second time and join forces with Character C. Together they fight against Character A.

There is nothing that says a plot can have only a single conflict triangle. A compelling novel or script will have several conflict triangles occurring simultaneously. Character A can be involved in two or three struggles simultaneously. The first will be the main plot and the others can be part of the main storyline or subplots.

Plotting example

Let's engage in an exercise to illustrate how a plot can come together.

Chris, the protagonist, has a treasure map and he's determined to find the treasure. Getting it is the plot problem.

Jack, the antagonist, knows about the treasure and the map and he's determined to get it before Chris does. This is the plot's beginning or the inciting incident.

After some thought, you decide on the ending: Chris will find and take the treasure. The graphical representation of the plot at this point looks like this.

The problem you face is filling in all the blank space between the beginning and the end. In short, you need a plot path. To put it a different way, you are now dealing with the plot cloud issue.

To complicate matters, you add another character, Ann, an FBI agent, who believes the treasure is loot from a bank robbery. Ann's story can be a subplot or part of the main storyline. Now the diagram looks like this.

The problem you now have is to figure out how to get the characters to the location of the treasure. After some thought, you decide Chris and Jack will move toward the treasure and bump into each other on the way.

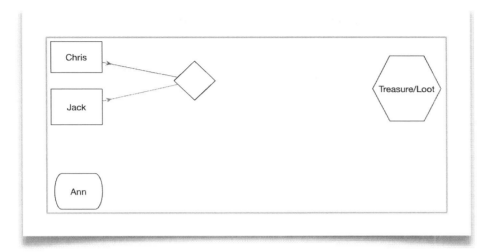

After more thought, you come up with another plot event: Jack and
Ann will collide as they both move toward the treasure.

The events at Points 1 and 2 have to be action scenes. The characters
have to do more than hide from each other or wave a hand in greeting.
There has to be action: a fistfight, a gun battle, a car chase (or a horse
chase if it's a Western). Something dramatic has to happen. Something to
show conflict tension and emotions. This is your chance to show the reader
your writing chops.

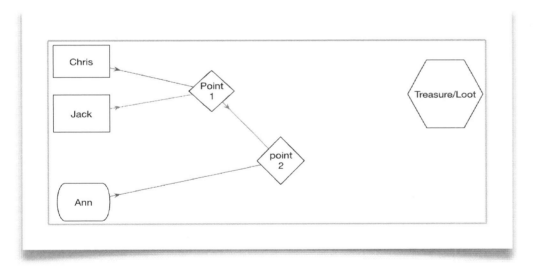

After the conflict at Points 1 and 2, the plot gets tricky. Your next job
is to get Chris, Jack and Ann to the location of the treasure. But *they all
have to arrive at the same time*. This requires a bit of planning to ensure

that the timing of the characters' journey is in sync so one of them doesn't arrive too early or too late.

Once they all arrive, you've reached the climax of your story. It won't be much of a climax if Chris arrives, gets the treasure and leaves before Jack gets there, finds out the treasure is gone and leaves before Ann shows up. Sequential arrivals won't cut it. That could happen in real life, but this is fiction, not real life.

Once the characters get to the treasure/loot location you have the set-up for a great amount of conflict. You can have Chris versus Jack; Chris versus Ann; Jack versus Ann; Ann versus both of the guys. You can have Chris and Ann team up against Jack. You can have Chris and Jack join forces against Ann or even Jack and Ann against Chris. However you arrange the conflicts and the ending, remember you also need tension and emotions.

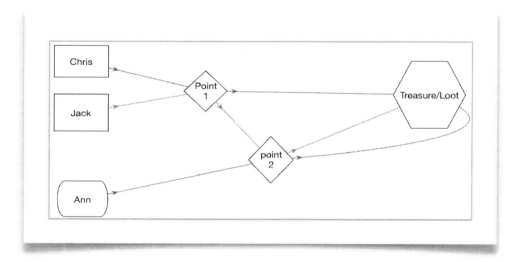

Once the conflicts are resolved, you need one more scene. You have to tell the reader what the winner gets for all the trouble he or she went through. Does Chris get the treasure and go off to live the good life? Or does he do something different with it? Whatever you decide, you have to tell the readers about it.

Although your ending has Chris coming out the winner, other endings are possible. Does Jack get the treasure and use it to fund a decadent life style? Does Ann recover the loot and get a promotion? Do all three die in a blaze of gunfire? Does the building then burn down making the bodies unidentifiable and leaving nothing but a mystery behind?

This plot example can be used in a number of variations. If the treasure is replaced by Chris' kidnapped daughter, you have a completely different story. If you write mystery stories, the treasure may be the point where all the clues come together to resolve the mystery.

Chapter 7: Subplots

HQ: Now that you've mastered how to build a plot, we can move on to understanding and developing subplots.

Author: More plot stuff?

HQ: Don't whine. It's unbecoming.

Author: Why do I need subplots? I have a great plot I'm going to use.

HQ: Subplots have a number of uses. I'll go into those uses next.

Author: Do I really have to make a subplot?

HQ: Yes you do. For a short story, one subplot may be sufficient. For a longer work like a novel, three or four or even more can be developed and should be considered.

Author: I guess I'll listen.

HQ: That's the spirit.

Purpose

Subplots have a number of uses. Here is a list of the main ones.

> Distract the reader from the main conflict.
>
> Give the reader a break.
>
> Stretch out the tension.
>
> Build anticipation.
>
> Explore and develop other characters.
>
> Provide foreshadowing.

Let's explore each one in more depth.

Distracting the reader is a device that can be used in many stories. While the reader is engrossed in the subplot, the sneaky main characters are off doing something that will surprise the reader when she finds out what they did.

Give the reader a break: If the plot is especially intense, the readers will appreciate a break. The subplot gives them a chance to catch their breath and cool off a bit before they plunge back into the main plot.

Stretch out the tension: The subplots also make the main plot seem longer, stretching out the tension.

Build anticipation: This stretching out with subplots will build the anticipation of the reader to reach the climax.

Explore and develop other characters: The subplots can be used to explore less important characters and give the readers insights into these characters.

Provide foreshadowing: A subplot can be used to show a development that seemingly is independent of the main plot, but is actually a crucial element in the climactic scenes.

Subplot example

Here is an example of a simple subplot suitable for a short story. Jim is the protagonist in the story and Harry is Jim's sidekick After the story gets going and the reader is acquainted with both men, Jim says, "Harry, what's up? You look like something is bothering you."

"It's my mother, Jim. She had a heart attack last night and she's in intensive care."

A scene or two later.

"How's your mother doing?" Jim asked.

"Gonna have open heart surgery this afternoon," Harry replied.

"Oh, man. I hope she comes through all right."

Another scene or two passes.

"Is your mother okay?" Jim asked.

"She's great." Harry grinned at his friend. "The operation was a success. She'll be home within a week."

Harry and his mother's problem is a full subplot even though we never meet the mother. It characterizes Harry by showing his concern for her health. It characterizes Jim by demonstrating his sympathy for Harry's situation.

More subplot stuff

Subplots shouldn't stop the main plot from going forward. By this I mean, don't insert an entire five-thousand-word subplot in between two main plot scenes. The subplot scenes should be spaced out and interwoven with the main plot and other subplots. A complicated subplot can run for the entire length of the main plot or a simpler subplot can wrap up during a single part of the story.

The subplots can involve less important characters or they can involve the main characters. In this latter case, the protagonist will have two or even three problems to work on. This can lead to overload for the character and greatly increase the tension and his emotional upheaval.

Subplots must be handled in a way that interweaves them with the main plot. In many cases, the subplot will impact on the main plot's development and either hinder or help that development.

Nesting

Subplots have a structure; they can't just be thrown into the story any which way the author feels like it. If you have more than one subplot you have to categorize them from most important to least important. The subplots are then nested within the main story line. This nesting arrangement is depicted in the diagram with Subplot A as the most important and Subplot C as the least important.

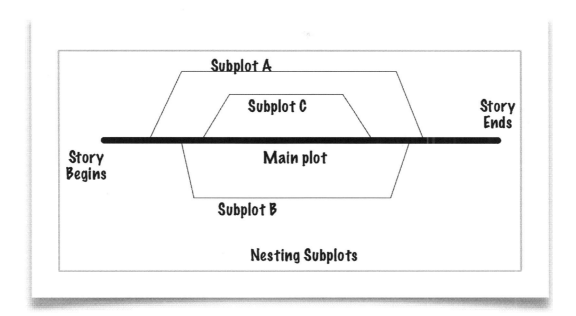

Here is a description on how the nesting would be implemented in the above diagram.

In the diagram, the heavy black line represents story time, i.e., time within the story as experienced by the characters. This line also represents the main plot.

After the characters are introduced and the plot problem recognized, a scene from Subplot A can be added. After a number of scenes from the main plot and an occasional one from Subplot A, Subplot B is introduced. More Main plot scenes are broken up by scenes from Subplots A and B. Then Subplot C is begun. Now the bulk of the story continues with the subplot scenes dropped in to break up the Main plot.

When the story approaches the climax, Subplot C is finished first. The Main plot continues and Subplot B is closed out. The Main plot moves closer to the climax and Subplot A is finished up. Now the way is clear for the reader (and the author) to concentrate on the story's climax.

It is not good form to have a subplot continue beyond the climactic scene from the main storyline. Once the climax is reached and the valida-tion scene shown, the story is over: the reader will no longer be interested in the outcome of a subplot. This means the validation scene is the end of the story. Don't keep adding scenes.

Chapter 8: Scene Design

Hank Quense: Now we come to an important area called scene design. This is where you'll spend much of your time after you finish up the characters and the plot.

Author: Scene design? I thought I just had to write stuff and call it a scene. There's more to it than that?

HQ: There's a lot more to it than just writing a few paragraphs. Scenes have to be designed and there are mandatory requirements in their design. Stories don't consist of paragraphs or chapters, they consist of scenes. Scenes are the building blocks of any story. To create a story, you have to create scenes.

Author: But what about chapters? Aren't they important too?

HQ: Actually, chapters aren't that important. Think of a chapter as a convenient bucket to hold a number of scenes.

Author: That's odd. Chapters always seemed so important to me. Every book I've ever read has the chapter headings in big letters, but those books say nothing about the scenes.

HQ: Remember this. A story is made up of scenes. Not paragraphs and not chapters; scenes.

Author: Hmm. That's food for thought and a different way of thinking about my story.

Scene design elements

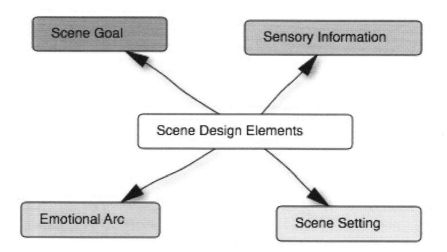

There are four elements that go into designing a scene. These are depicted in the graphic. Sensory information is good to have but isn't absolutely necessary.

Scene setting is more important than sensory information. Both the emotional arc and the scene goal are mandatory.

In Chapter 1, I discussed the importance of giving readers the information to allow them to build images. Sensory information and scene setting are the tools to do that.

I'll address each element in the sections that follow.

In an appendix, you'll find an annotated scene from one of my short stories. It illustrates how all four elements can be worked into a scene.

Scenes need a structure to keep them from rambling on and on *ad infinitum*. The scene should be restricted to a specific time. The scene should be restricted to a specific location. For example, if a scene takes place in a schoolyard basketball court, a different scene should be developed to continue the action that night in a tavern. Similarly, if a scene involves Jim who is in Manhattan, a second scene will be required to involve Sam who is in Denver.

The scene must accomplish one of several purposes. It must characterize someone or pass vital information to the reader or it must move the story closer to the climax. If the scene accomplishes none of these, it should be deleted since all it does is add to the word count without accomplishing anything useful.

Sensory Information.

We're surrounded by stuff our senses pick up. The sight and colors in a rainbow or a camp fire. The look on the face of a delighted child. The smell of newly mown grass. The sound of traffic or the sound of birds or heavy metal bands. The touch of a child's hand or a smack in the face. The feel of a kiss or the thrill of a hug.

These are all part of being alive. They are part of our humanity. So, your job as a writer is to make sure the reader shares the sensory information that the characters experience.

Sight is always shared with readers; it's how the character tells the reader what's going on in the scene. But that isn't enough. If the scene is in a room with a fireplace, how does the smoke smell? Is the fireplace burning logs from an apple tree? Does the smoke hurt the character's throat? If the scene is in a wooded area, is there the sound of small animals scurrying around in the underbrush? Birdsong? Chattering of squirrels? How about the earthy smell of decomposing leaves? If the scene is set in Manhattan the reader has to "hear" the rumble of traffic, the piercing scream of fire engine sirens, the staccato sounds of construction.

Without sensory information, the scene will seem sterile to the reader.

Scene setting

The scene setting is a subset of the story setting. If the setting of your story is the Sahara Desert, then scenes can be set on a sand dune, at an oasis, in a sand storm, at a deserted fort.

The important issue here is that you give the reader the words necessary to build an image of the scene setting.

Besides the location, the setting details can include the weather and the season, the time of day (or night) and any other pertinent information. However, there is a danger of overdoing these details. For example, the weather doesn't have to be mentioned in every scene, especially if a number of scenes take place in the same area around the same time.

To help describe the scene setting and to be able to relate the details, I advise making a sketch. That's what I do. If a setting is used only once, I make a quick sketch on a piece of scrap paper then throw it out when I'm done. If the setting is one that will be used a number of times during the course of the story, I make the sketch on my computer and stash it in a file where I can open it to refresh my memory about the details. If the fireplace is on the left side of the room in one scene, it won't do to move it to the right side in a subsequent scene. Readers will catch your mistake.

Here is a sketch I made for a recent novel. I had two reasons for making this sketch. First, I had no idea what the scroll library looked like when I began. So making the drawing told me everything I needed to know to write the scene. Second, the room was used in several scenes and I wanted to make sure I didn't inadvertently move something.

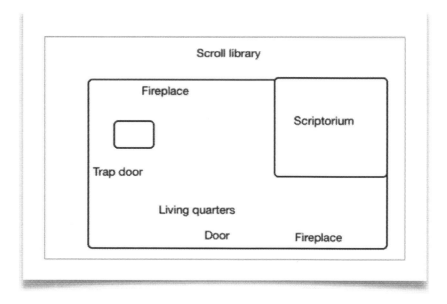

Scene goal

The purpose of a story is to take the reader on a journey. That journey is made up of scenes. A short story may have six to ten scenes, while an average-sized novel may demand one-hundred-fifty scenes. The basic requirement for these scenes is that it characterizes someone or passes on relevant information or moves the reader closer to the journey's end: the story's climax.

To satisfy this requirement the scene must have a goal. The scene can't simply be a collection of paragraphs clumped together for the author's convenience.

For simplicity, we will concentrate on scenes that move the reader closer to the story's climax.

In a short story, the scene goal is usually related to solving the plot problem. In a novel, the scene goal can be related to a number of objectives.

Typical examples of scene goals are to get vital information, to reach a specific location, to identify someone. These goals are waypoints in the movement of the story. Some scene goals may be accomplished within a single scene or the goal may require several scenes before it is reached or completed. For instance, to reach the specific location can take many scenes, each one moving the characters closer to the location.

A goal such as this (reaching a location) can be the objective of an entire part of the story involving a number of chapters. Many of the scenes will involve overcoming obstacles such as werewolves or a rain-swollen river or a holiday traffic jam. In a quest story, reaching the location can be the goal of the entire story.

The important message here is this: no matter how many scenes it takes, each scene must have a goal. If the scene doesn't advance the story the scene should be deleted. All the scene does in this case is to take up space for no purpose.

Since the scenes are supposed to move the reader towards the climax, it stands to reason that the scene goals should be nested into the story goal (in the case of a short story) or into the goal for a portion of the story (in a longer work). For instance, the scene goal in act two of the story should move the reader toward act two's goal and the act two goal should be a waypoint of the ultimate story goal.

Here is a graphic to depict this situation.

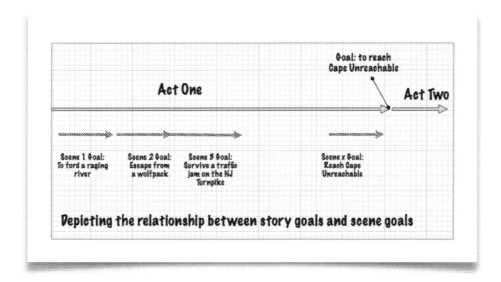

In this example, the goal of act one is to reach Cape Unreachable. Achieving this objective will open the way to move toward the goal of act two. Both of these objectives will take the reader closer to the story's climax.

Emotional arc

Readers want to experience and share the characters' emotional journey. In order to create this emotional journey, each scene must have an emotional change in it. What this means is that the character's emotion at the end of the scene must be changed from the character's emotion at the start of the scene. Whether the change is positive or negative is irrelevant. A scene with a flat emotional arc is not a good scene.

An additional requirement is that the character's emotional change in a scene must be linked to the *ending* emotion in the previous scene and become the *beginning* emotion in the succeeding scene. In other words, the emotional changes form a continuous arc that stretches from the story's opening scene to the climatic scene at the end. Stories with multiple main characters will have multiple emotional arcs, one for each main character.

A simple example of this is illustrated below.

In this scenario, the starting emotion for Scene Y is the same as the ending emotion in Scene X. And Scene Z picks up where Scene Y left off. This example is for a single character. With multiple main characters and emotional arcs, this continuous arc shown would be interrupted by the scenes from the other emotional arcs. Thus, keeping track of each character's emotional arc is yet another chore for the author.

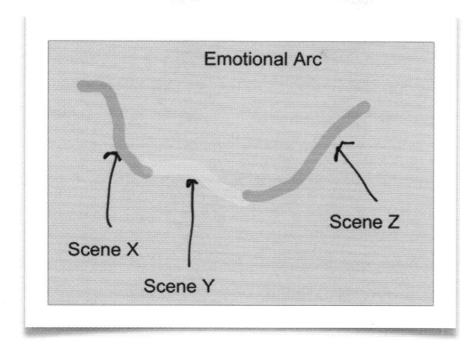

For a short story, developing this arc is relatively simple because of the small number of scenes involved. The situation is more complicated in a long story because of the many scenes involved and the multiple points of view and subplots.

Let's simplify this mind-boggling concept. The emotional arc I'll describe belongs to a single character, not the entire cast. However, each major character needs his own emotional arc. Yeah, that's right. Both the antagonist and the protagonist need an emotional arc. The sidekicks can and should have one also, especially if they star in their own subplots.

Further, the main characters can have more than one emotional arc. For instance, the hero can have an emotional arc for the main plot and another emotional arc for a subplot. The subplot emotional arc will be different from the main plot emotional arc, although there could be an overlap and even reinforcement of one arc or the other.

As an example of emotional arcs, in my *Wotan's Dilemma*, the main character, the Valkyrie Brunnhilde, struggles to understand mortal love. This is her main objective during the story. But her need to attain this knowledge puts her in conflict with Wotan's order to kill her favorite mortal. Thus, her inner emotional need — understanding mortal love — and her outer emotional need — to obey Wotan's command — set up an intense conflict that she has to deal with. And the two emotional needs are mutually exclusive. This is the stuff of a gripping emotional battle that readers love.

Chapter 9: Plot and Emotional Arcs

Hank Quense: Okay, now we get into some pretty heavy stuff.

Author: Deeper than the stuff we've already gone through?

HQ: Yeah. Remember the emotional arcs we discussed in the last chapter?

Author: Sure. That wasn't so long ago.

HQ: And remember in Chapter 6 we discussed how the plot had to move the reader toward the climax?

Author: Yeah, but why do I think you're about to unleash some really weird concept?

HQ: I am about to unleash another concept, but it isn't weird. It's essential to building a credible climax.

Author. (Sigh) I suppose I'm ready.

HQ: Great. Let's do it. To take pity on you, I've prepared a lot of graphics to help explain this new concept.

Author: (Groan)

Plot and emotional arc

In the chapter on scene design, I explained the concept of a continuous emotional arc that runs through a number of scenes. That emotional connection has a very important role to play in the development of the story.

The story's emotional arc is a product of the scene designs melded to the plot events. The purpose of the emotional arc is to grip the reader and keep her reading even though it's past her bedtime.

To explain this concept, I'll use a series of graphs to illustrate the emotional changes as the story progresses.

To begin, here is the basic structure of the graph. As you see, the vertical axis is used to record the character's emotional state, both positive and negative, while the horizontal axis shows time within the story.

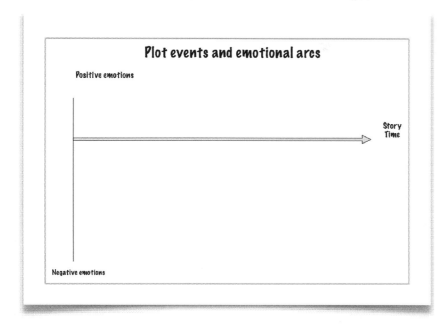

In the next chart the red line depicts the emotional curve you'll find in stories created by new writers. Essentially, it's a flat line, an indication of little if any emotional changes in the story. For contrast, my emotional curve for the first draft is shown in green. It's much steeper than the red line, but it can still use some sharpening and improvement. That's what second and third drafts are for; improving the emotional curve (and fixing typos among other chores).

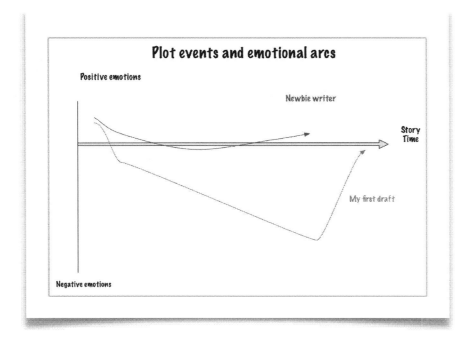

With the basics out of the way, we can now construct an emotional curve as your story unfolds. I'll explain this one step at a time. In the next chart, the story begins with the protagonist in a positive emotional state. Life is good, he's cool, everything is grand.

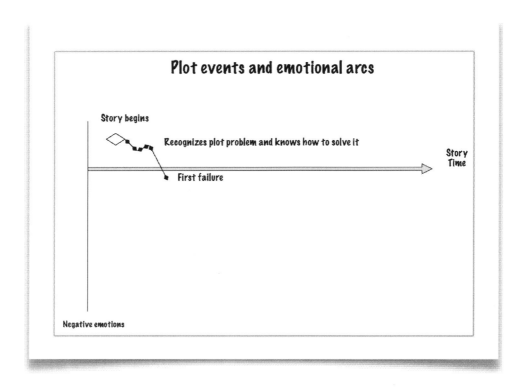

Then he recognizes the plot problem and his emotional state drops a bit lower. He's not quite as happy as he was. "Why me?" he moans. "I don't have time for this stuff." But then he thinks of a way to solve the problem and his emotional state improves. He puts his plan into action and it fails. "Uh-oh, this isn't as easy I thought it would be." This failure results in a drop in his emotional state.

He ponders the situation and comes up with another plan.

His second attempt also fails and now he's getting alarmed. His emotional state plunges deeper into negative territory.

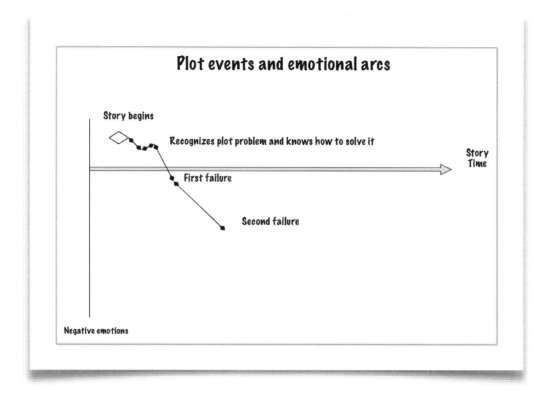

These attempts can be a single scene or they can involve a number of scenes, but each scene has to result in a lowering of the emotional state. Struggling on, he develops still another plan and executes it.

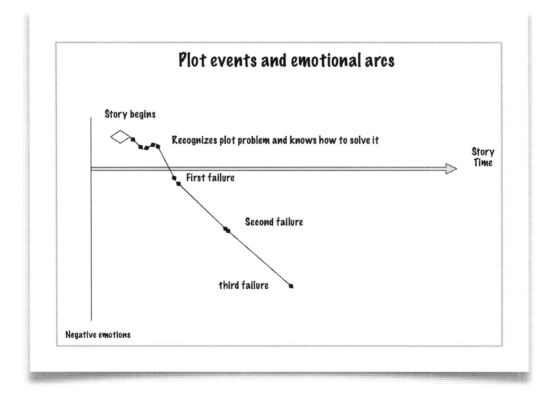

Again he fails and his emotional state has now sunk into depression. After wallowing around for a while, he sucks it up and decides he'll solve the problem or die trying. At this point, your story has reached the beginning of the climax.

I'm sure you've watched a movie that had you on the edge of your seat toward the end. You're biting your nails wondering how the hero can get out of the mess he's in. In this case, the director has set you up for the movie's big climatic scene. That's what you, the author, must do with your story and the readers. You have to get the readers anxious to find out how the hero will survive/solve/whatever the next scene.

As the hero struggles through the climactic scene, his emotional state soars (or not, if he doesn't succeed, which is always an option).

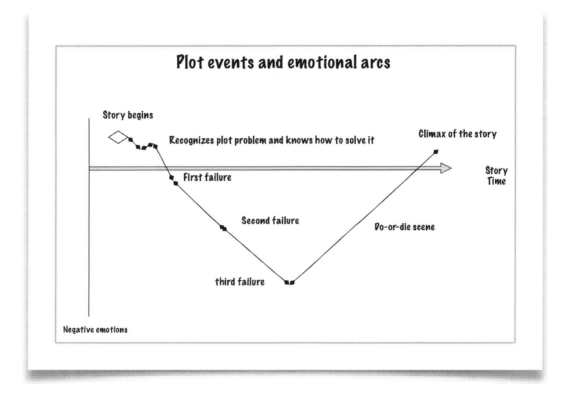

Don't forget, the climactic scene must be followed by the validation scene.

The charts presented here depict the hero's emotional journey. The bad guy also has an emotional journey and it's the exact opposite of the good guy's journey. Every time the protagonist fails, the antagonist wins and his emotional state shoots up while the protagonist's falls.

This overall process of constructing an emotional arc is how a compelling story is put together. Whether you draw a chart, use an outline or a mind-map, you have to track these emotional changes in order to properly develop the story's emotional arc.   It won't do to have the protag's emotional arc bounce around and go positive before the story's ending. The protag's emotions can improve and tick upward (slightly) but this has to be a temporary situation and his downward spiral must continue soon afterward.

For a short story, each of the failures can be a scene. In a longer work, each failure can be one or more chapters long or even an entire act.

Part 3: Storytelling
Chapter 10: Basic Storytelling

Hank Quense: After a lot of work, you've come up with a bunch of creative ideas and you've finished the story design. So all you have to do is write the story. Right?

Author: Yeah, I'm ready to go. Thanks for all your help. I'll take it from here.

HQ: I'm not done and neither are you. We have more chapters to go through.

Author: Hey, I'm finished with the design work, so on to the first draft. I'm good to go.

HQ: Listen to me. No matter how great your ideas are and no matter how great your characters and plot are, if you don't tell the story in a way that is appealing to the readers, no one will read your story. If your story can't hold the readers' attention all your creativity and design work is wasted.

Author: Wait! I have to wade through more of your stuff?

HQ: We have tons of stuff to go over. Almost all of it concerns storytelling techniques. This is the stuff that keeps the readers turning the pages instead of cleaning the house. Or mowing the lawn. Or going to the movies.

Author: Do I have to?

HQ: Yes and don't whine.

Tense

One of the initial decisions an author must make is what tense to use in the story. Most nonfiction utilizes the present tense as does this book. Most fiction uses the past tense, although a number of fiction books now use the present tense. In all my novels I use the past tense. It just feels like the correct way to tell the story. Reading a present tense novel doesn't seem right to me. It's like there is something that needs to be fixed or redone.

In telling a story, there are other tenses that could be used such as the future tense. This could be a time traveler relating what will happen in the future. I think stories that use unusual tenses will initially surprise and intrigue a reader, but they will quickly lose their luster and end up turning the reader off.

I recommend using the past tense. The past tense is so common it's almost invisible to the reader. This invisibility makes it easy for the reader to slip comfortably into the story and will in no way interfere with the readers' enjoyment.

Cause and Effect

I once critiqued a short story in which the protagonist used a sword hidden in his cane to dispatch the bad guy at the climax. Unfortunately, the character never used a cane in any scene prior to the climatic ending. In this case, the author used an *effect* without a *cause*.

While coincidences are a part of reality, they have no place in fiction. If something happens in a story, there has to be a reason, a cause for it to happen. In the example above, the author should have shown the protagonist limping along and using the cane long before the climax.

Think of the *effects* as plot events. Every plot event has to have a *cause* prior to the event happening. On the other hand, if you list a *cause*, you have to ensure it has an *effect*. Otherwise, the reader will be baffled about the orphaned *cause*.

Stimulus and reaction

Stimuli and reactions are the basic couplet of actions in a story. It's cause and effect done small. It's a simple principle and easy to understand, yet the couplet is often done incorrectly and this leads to confusion for the reader.

The correct sequence for the couplet is 1) a stimulus occurs and 2) a reaction follows. Despite the simplicity of this formula, the components are often reversed or even worse, one of the components is omitted.

What is a stimulus? It can be a punch, a kiss, a dirty look or a pistol shot to give a few examples. It's a "happening."

What is a reaction? It can be a defensive move, a sense of surprise, returning a dirty look or diving behind a barrel.

I often see examples in which the reaction occurs before the stimulus. Even worse, the writer describes a character's reaction but omits the stimulus. I'll bet you've read stories in which a character does something and you stop reading because you know you missed something. Rereading a few paragraphs doesn't fill in the blank space. The problem is the author omitted the stimulus and left you trying to figure out why the reaction occurred.

A popular version of this broken couplet is, "*Character A smiled/ grinned/growled etc.*" In these cases, the author doesn't bother telling us why Character A did what he did.

Let's examine this basic concept in more detail using examples.

Jody panicked. This is a reaction minus a stimulus

Jody panicked. A dead body lay on the floor. This is better, but the reaction precedes the stimulus. Readers will probably accept this sequence because the two components are so closely related.

A dead body lay on the floor. Jody panicked. This is the correct sequence for the couplet.

Here are some additional couplet violations.

John dived behind a barrel. A shot rang out. Here the reaction occurs before the stimulus.

Sally threw a drink in Alex's face. This is a reaction, but no stimulus is shown, unless the stimulus occurred in preceding sentences and this is a delayed reaction. It is also possible that Sally and Alex have great deal of history which is the stimulus for Sally's reaction

A bike ran over her foot. Definitely a stimulus but without a reaction.

To tell the truth, I often violate the stimulus/reaction couplet sequence in my first drafts. I correct them in my second or third drafts.

Using the correct sequence in the couplet is a basic storytelling technique you have to master.

Foreshadowing

Foreshadowing is a useful device in which the author plants clues or hints. The Wikipedia definition says: *Foreshadowing or guessing ahead is a literary device by which an author hints what is to come.[1] It is used to avoid disappointment. It is also sometimes used to arouse the reader.*

There is an old stage play adage that goes like this: If you need a gun in the last scene, you'd better show the gun to the audience in the first scene. Audiences and readers don't like stories that have characters using stuff the author never told them about, like the gun above.

As an example of foreshadowing, in my latest novel *Moxie's Decision* I had Moxie fight a duel with knitting needles in a climactic scene. In order to set up that scene, I showed Moxie knitting with two of her maids early in the book. In the middle of the book Moxie is training to fight with swords, spears and other pointy objects. She recollects her days knitting and thinks she could now use the needles as weapons. These two references to the knitting needles sets up the duel at the end and the reader isn't surprised by Moxie's use of the needles. This is also an example of cause and effect.

You can also use material from the character's biography to foreshadow important events later in the story. As an example of this, suppose a character has a fear of open water such as a lake or the sea. This fear is based an event when he was a five-year-old. Back then, the character almost drowned. At the climax of the story, the character is faced with a situation in which he has to save a person drowning in a lake. Does the character overcome his fear of water and save the person? Or does he walk away and hope no one saw him? Of course, to use this foreshadowing, the author has to show the character's fear of water early in the story and explain it.

Another example is a fear of dark places such as caves or unlit basements. This fear could be based on a traumatic childhood experience. Naturally, the story's climax requires the character to master his fear and go into a cave.

Using a storytelling technique like this can greatly increase the reader's enjoyment, but the adage above holds true. You can't have a character's fear first show up at a tense moment near the end. The reader has to be shown the character's fear early on and the reader has to understand what caused it before it can be used effectively in the climax.

Foreshadowing can also be used to mislead the reader. In a mystery story, if you show a character acting suspicious, the reader will assume she has identified the guilty party. At the end, surprise the reader by revealing a different culprit. This device is widely used in mystery stories.

Dialog and exposition

An author can pass information to the reader in one of two ways. The author can have characters discuss or argue about a situation and, in the course of the dialog, insert the information. Internal monologue is the second way. In this situation, the author chooses to tell the reader about it using exposition.

In the reader's viewpoint, dialog is more interesting than internal monologue and exposition. In most cases, the dialog choice will require more words. The chapter introductions in this book were exposition at one time. I felt these introductions were flat and uninteresting so I changed them to dialog and the word count for each introduction increased about twenty-five percent. These dialog introductions also became more interesting. (I think.)

Of course, if the author needs to enter a character's mind and engage in internal monologue, this has to be exposition. An exception could be made if the character suffers from multiple personalities. In this case, the different personalities could hold an internal conversation to discuss a situation.

While exposition is necessary, it should be limited whenever it can. This is especially true when it comes to info dumps. Info dumps are those deadly, dense passages filled with information the author thinks the reader has to know. Perhaps the reader does need to know this stuff, but an info dump ensures the material will not be read. It won't be read because many, many readers skip info dumps and flip through the pages until they come to a more interesting part.

See the section on world-building in Chapter 14 for further discussion on info dumps.

One effective use for exposition is employed at the beginning of scenes to describe the scene setting.

Telling and showing

Many instructors and books on writing urge writers to "show" the story to the reader rather than "telling" it. This is absurd. The vast majority of every book is "telling." Showing certainly is something that an author should use, but its use has to be judicious. If a writer uses too much showing the reader will get bored and stop reading.

As an example of too much showing, consider this example:

Jane stripped off her pajamas, yawned a few times, scratched her butt, turned on the shower and adjusted the hot water. Once it was satisfactory, she entered the shower, got wet and started to soap up. After that she washed her hair. Then she just stood and let the hot water course over her body soothing her muscles and relaxing her entire body and mood. She toweled off and dried her hair with the dryer. Naked, she went to her walk-in closet and selected her outfit for the day. After rejecting a few items, she chose tan jeans and a dark brown jersey.

Next came her makeup. She carefully matched the eyeliner color with the lipstick and blush colors. Satisfied with the result she went to the kitchen, brewed a cup of coffee and drank it while watching a morning news show.

After rinsing the cup and placing it in the dishwasher, she grabbed her bag and left for work.

That's an example of showing.

The author can accomplish the same result by telling: *Jane showered, dressed, drank a cup of coffee and left for work.*

The telling example is much simpler and faster. The showing example is long and boring. Why does the reader have to see Jane's morning ritual What relevancy does it have to the story line and plot? In Chapter 8, I listed the uses of a scene. They were: characterize someone, pass on information or move the story closer to the climax. In the showing example, the scene does none of these things. Unless Jane is a professional shower-taker and is prepping for a crucial match. In other words if you "show" the character performing mundane chores as in this example, your story will bog down in dull non-action.

If you look at the word count for both examples, the showing example took one-hundred-sixty-one words and the telling example twelve. Quite a difference.

Extrapolate these numbers to a book filled with unnecessary showing and you'll see that the story can get overwhelmed with trivial details.

Showing definitely is a technique that a writer should master, but one has to be careful how it is used. There are many opportunities for "showing" in any story. The writer simply has to understand how to use them and how to spot opportunities.

Let's try a few more examples.

Brunnhilde nervously looked at her watch.

In this example, the author directly tells the reader what Brunnhilde's emotional state is.

Brunnhilde shredded a paper napkin, fidgeted on her chair and glanced at her watch.

In this case, the author doesn't tell the reader what Brunnhilde's emotional state is. Instead the author depicts a woman acting nervously. It's up to the reader to decipher the words to determine Brunnhilde's emotional state. And readers love to do this.

In this rather simple example, I've illustrated the power of showing. It engages the reader and gets her involved in the story. The reader is now saying to herself, "Oh, dear. Brunnhilde is nervous about something. I wonder what is bothering her?" In the first example the reader doesn't have to do this because the author told her about Brunnhilde's state.

Here's another example.

Margo reacted angrily.

As before, the author tells the reader about the character's mental state

Margo scowled, placed her hands on her hips and stamped her foot.

Here, the reader has to interpret the author's words to understand what is happening. Of course, the reader can always misinterpretation the meaning. Instead of thinking Margo is angry, the reader may decide Margo sees and kills a cockroach. Nothing in this life is perfect. In this example, we see that showing takes more words than telling.

He entered the room hesitantly.

The use of an adverb is often an indication of an action that can be converted to showing. The sentence above can be rewritten to show a guy walking hesitantly.

"Help me," she said imploringly.

A dialog tag and an adverb is *always* telling and should be replaced with showing. Here you should show the woman sobbing and pleading as she says, "Help me."

Using showing as I've done in these examples will make for much more powerful writing and much more reader enjoyment. It will take practice to get comfortable with spotting and replacing instances of telling. However it will be worth the effort. Go for it!

Central metaphor

A central metaphor will change an ordinary story into something special. It is a recurring image that a character uses throughout the story. However, it is not easy to build a new one for each story. Sometimes I can't come up with one no matter how hard I try. Sometimes the only one I can think of is one I've already used and I don't want to repeat the central metaphor in another novel. Perhaps the concept is best illustrated by showing some examples from my stories.

1: A low-ranking alien officer struggles to get ahead on her ability in a military society that views assassination and treachery as the preferred method of advancement. She pictures herself as a ship of sanity sailing on a sea of madness searching for a safe harbor. Later on, when she faces difficulties, she imagines her ship careening toward a rocky shore. After another setback, she sees her unarmed ship of sanity being pursued by a pirate fleet. This is the central metaphor from my novel *Zaftan Miscreants*.

2: A young roaming bailiff sets out on his first law-enforcement mission and imagines himself to be an eagle leaving the nest for its initial flight. After a screwup, he wonders if young eagles make mistakes. After a second botched assignment, he asks himself how a young eagle would go about covering its tracks. This novella is called *Chasing Dreams* and was published in *Tales From Gundarland*.

A few references to the character's image will have the reader buying-in to the metaphor. *Just don't overdo it* by bringing up the central metaphor in every scene.

Crisis management

Let's say that in the course of a scene your character runs into a terrifying situation. Getting the character into these situations is easy. Getting him out is not so easy and you also have to deal with the emotional trauma involved. You can show the character getting away from whatever is so terrifying, perhaps by backing out of the immediate area, but you still can't ignore the strong emotion the character experienced. Your character has gone through a terrifying emotional change; you have to show that emotion getting dissipated.

I'll use an event in a recent short story of mine as an example. The character Leofric runs into a squad of hostile archers:

"Stand or die," a snarling voice said from Leofric's left. He turned and faced a notched arrow pointing at his head. A surge of fear spread upward from Leofric's groin. Six other archers emerged from the trees. Each wore a forest green jerkin and hose. The one who spoke had a hood on his jerkin. Pulled forward, it hid his face in shadows. Leofric froze and almost stopped breathing. He wondered who the archers were and what they intended to do.

"Now then," the first archer said. "Let's begin the trial. Me name is Jackey and this is me patch of land. Trespass at your peril. Are you Norman scum?"

"I . . . never met a Norman," Leofric said. He turned his head slightly so he could see all the archers with his peripheral vision. He couldn't figure

a way to get out of this mess without getting killed. At this short range, the arrows couldn't miss.

"You a Welsh raider?"

"No," Leofric replied.

"A murderer onna run?"

"No."

"A priest or a monk?" The archer slightly eased the tension on the bowstring and Leofric's fear lessened a notch.

"No."

"A lawyer?"

Leofric shook his head.

Jackey shifted his feet and sighed. Leofric thought he might get out of this situation alive.

"Well, if you ain't any of them things, you can use me forest." Jackey pointed the arrow at the ground.

Leofric gulped air and let his taut muscles relax.

As you can see, I showed Leofric's great fear evaporating as the archer became less hostile. In other words, I defused Leofric's crisis. If I didn't, the reader would be left wondering what happened to the great fear Leofric experienced.

To summarize, you can't place your character in a traumatic situation and simply ignore his intense emotional response. You have to defuse those emotions before your character moves on. If you don't, you'll leave the reader wondering what happened and that's never a good thing.

Voice

Every individual has a number of voices they use interchangeably. Depending on the situation and who they're talking to, they may use a stern voice, a commanding voice, or a pleasant voice.

You don't think about which voice to use, it just happens and you can switch between voices at will. Listen to a child at play. If she is playing at being a parent, her voice will be quite different from the voice she uses when she's cuddling a puppy or playing doctor with her doll. In these cases, the child is of course imitating adults, but it demonstrates the various voices we all use.

Well, if we have different voices, don't our characters have to have different voices as well? If your character is angry, he must use an angry voice and it has to be different from his happy voice. As you tell your story, you'll have to have your characters employ a number of voices to make them sound realistic.

Most people when they switch voices also switch vocabularies. When using an angry voice, a character may resort to swear words. When lecturing someone, the vocabulary will use more erudite words.

Chapter 11: Point of view

Hank Quense: Are you ready to tackle the most technical aspect of storytelling?

Author: This is a trick question, right?

HQ: Nope. It's a legit question. We're about to discuss point of view and it is technical.

Author: Technical as in math or physics?

HQ: Nothing like that. When I started writing stories, I had never heard of point of view and didn't know what it was. A nice critiquer explained it to me. Why are you cringing?

Author: Can you give me a short description?

HQ: Sure. Point of view means who tells the story. Is it you, the author? Is it a character? Which one? More than one character?

Author: Huh? That doesn't sound so bad. Bring it on.

Point of view choices

You're the author. You created the story, the characters, the plot, the scenes. It's your baby. Now you have to make a choice about how the story is told to the reader.

In the old days, stories were told in the omniscient point of view. In other words, the author told the story. As a way of telling an entire story this mode is obsolete. In fact, for many readers, it's painful to read these stories. Any of Charles Dickens's stories can serve as an example. The characters and the plots are great, the storytelling is dull for today's readers.

Nowadays, it's common to use omniscient POV in a limited way such as describing the scene setting while most of the story is told in a character's POV. The most common point of view choice is third person limited and first person point of views.

Here are examples on how each type looks to the reader.

Omniscient: *The old forest was gloomy and humid. Not even a hint of a breeze stirred the leaves. Occasionally a small shaft of sunlight broke through and illuminated a small patch of ground. Vines hung from the lower limbs of the huge oak trees and thick spider webs filled in the spaces between vines and limbs.*

In this case the narrator is the author telling the reader what the forest looks like.

Third person limited: *Jack traveled through a gloomy forest. Already sweat soaked his shirt. Ahead, a small ray of sunshine somehow evaded the thick umbrella of oak limbs and shone on a pile of moldy leaves. Jack ducked under a vine hanging from a tree limb and sidestepped a thick spider web.*

Here we see the forest narrated by a character who uses actions and feelings to help the description: soaked shirt, ducking, sidestepping. This type of narrator brings the reader closer to the action than in the previous example.

First person: *I had a sense of foreboding about the gloomy forest. Even the small shaft of sunlight ahead didn't do anything to lighten my mood. Sweat ran down my nose and dripped on my already soaked shirt. I had to duck under a drooping vine to move ahead and edge around a thick spider web.*

This time, the description is even more personal and the reader is brought even closer to the forest. That is the consequence of using a first person narrator.

Deciding on a point of view, who the POV character is, and whether or not there will be multiple POV characters are important decisions an author has to make before starting to write the first draft. A first person story is quite different from a third person story and the difference isn't just in the pronouns used.

First person POV stories are highly restrictive in what the author can do and not do. Third person POV stories offer more flexibility and less limitations.

As an example of the choices facing an author, consider these third person point of view options. Your primary POV character can be the protagonist. This is the choice in many stories. An alternative is to use the antagonist as the primary POV character. In this case the story is told from the perspective of the bad guy, not the good guy. A third alternative is to use the protagonist's sidekick as the main POV character. The sidekick character now serves primarily as a narrator or a reporter, telling the reader what the protagonist is doing and how he is reacting to situations. If you take a single story and consider the implications of writing it from each of these three different POV characters, you will see that each instance will produce a story that is quite different from the other two.

If this same story is written using a first person POV choice the story will change even more.

As you can see, I've illustrated the problem facing the author; one story, four different narrator choices -- three third person and one first person — leading to the story being told in four different ways. Which decision is the best one? Each of the four point of view choices offers advantages and disadvantages to the author so there is no best decision. The author simply has to suck it up and choose how she wants the story to be told.

Whichever option the author chooses, that is the best one for her. There is no wrong choice here.

Omniscient point of view

Writing the story using the omniscient point of view is like playing god. You, the author, know everything, see everything and even know the future of the characters. You know what each character is thinking, what his mood is and what he plans to do.

This is pretty cool and it is the way most classic books were written. Charles Dickens, for instance, wrote almost entirely in the omniscient POV. This way of writing a story is obsolete now, but that doesn't mean omniscient POV isn't used. Actually it's used quite a bit, but usually in small doses such as the description of a setting at the beginning of a scene. After the omniscient narrator is finished describing the location, the author switches point of view to one of the characters.

In sci-fi and fantasy stories, as well as in other genres, the author feels compelled to share the world she has invented for her characters. This leads to the cringe-worthy info dump, pages and pages of detail about the world, its climate, its geological makeup and on and on and on until the reader is bored out of her skull. I skip all this nonsense when I read a book.

These info dumps are written in the omniscient POV and demonstrate the godlike power it gives the author since no character could or would know all this stuff. While the world-building material is often essential to the story, the info-dump isn't. The author must give the reader small doses of the world-building, doses that are small enough so that they don't interrupt the flow of the story.

To provide a graphical illustration on the omniscient POV refer to the diagram below.

You, the author are the eye at the top. Your all-seeing eyeball knows what each character is doing, where the car is going, who is driving it and how much mileage the car gets and you even know what is causing the strange noise in the transmission.

You can jump between characters to tell the reader what each character is thinking or what the character is about to do. You can even end a scene or a chapter with the dreaded, *"Little did they know . . ."*

One argument in favor of omniscient POV is its compactness. Other POV's will require more words to express the same information.

One of the problems with this type of POV is that it puts distance between the characters and the readers. Another fact is that a heavy dose of omniscience becomes boring as the author describes social, political or religious concerns. You can get a taste of this by reading an old classic novel written almost exclusively in the omniscient POV. *Tom Jones* by Henry Fielding is a good choice. Fielding constantly interrupts the narrative to tell side stories or to explore the life history of a new character or to give us a torrent of words on a current social or political issue. Still, many readers love these types of stories. I guess that is why they are called classics.

Third person point of view

To be clear, omniscient is a third person point of view but it is an unlimited third person viewpoint. In other words, there are no restrictions on the omniscient point of view. In this section I'll talk about a different third person point of view, a limited one. This is the most popular point of view and the majority of novels use it as the predominant point of view.

In this point of view scheme, the narrator is a character rather than the author. The scenes are related through the eyes and ears of a character. This POV character does NOT know what the other characters are thinking or what they are about to do. The POV character can guess the others emotional state by observing their speech and body language, but this POV character does not know what is going on in their minds. That is main difference between this viewpoint and the omniscient viewpoint.

Since the reader will be spending much time with the POV characters, the readers will get emotionally involved with these characters and that is a good thing. Readers want this involvement. They want to root for the good guys and hope for the worst for the bad guys. This emotional involvement is something that is difficult to do with omniscient POV because of the distance between the story and the reader.

This sketch depicts the limited third person point of view. Character X can see what the others are doing but has no way of knowing what they are thinking.

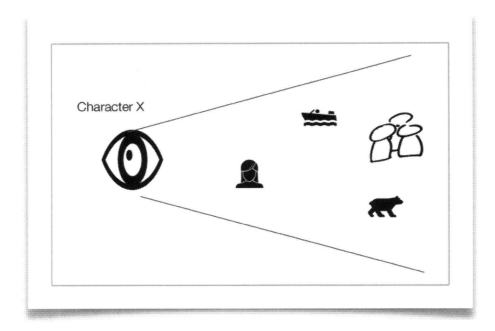

The secret to writing in this POV is for the author to get inside the POV character's mind and write the scene from there. Believe me, this is strange the first few times you try it, but after a while, it becomes quite natural. Of course, this POV scheme is restrictive. Unlike omniscient POV, this POV character can't know what is happening in the building across the street. In the beginning, there is a tendency for the inexperienced writer to break out of the POV character's mind to tell the reader stuff the POV character can't possibly know. Often, this will entail telling the reader what a different character is thinking or about to do. Trust me, readers may not understand the technical details of POV restrictions, but they know when it's done incorrectly.

Consider this major difference between third person omniscient and limited. Jack is a character in Manhattan. Sue is a character in San Francisco. Jack is going about his business in New York when an event that will impact on Jack occurs in San Francisco. With omniscience, the author simply tells us what happened out west. With third person limited, in order to describe the San Francisco event, the author has to switch from Jack's POV to Sue's POV. After describing the action, the readers know about it, but Jack doesn't. For Jack to learn about the event, Sue has to call him or Jack must see it on TV or read about it in the newspapers or on social media.

Another interesting aspect of this POV scheme is that the reader sees what the POV character thinks is happening, but what the character thinks is happening may not be reality. The events are filtered by the POV's tunnel vision.

Everyone suffers from tunnel vision to some degree. It's a set of personal filters that interpret or bend reality and sometimes greatly change what the character "thinks" he sees.

For example, three characters, Jack, Sue and Mary, are walking along the street when a car swerves out of control and smashes into a building a hundred feet ahead of them. Jack, a drug dealer, sees the crash as an assassination attempt. Sue, a nurse, sees a need for her medical assistance. Mary, a self-centered egotist, is annoyed because she'll now have to detour into the street to get around the wreck.

Situations like this can lead to a great deal of character confusion and tension. For instance, if each of the three characters starts talking to the other two about what just happened, none of the three will understand the others' interpretation of the event.

"Did you see that?" Jack exclaimed. "Someone tried to whack me!"

"I wish I had a medical kit," Sue said. "I'm sure someone is hurt and needs attention."

"I'll never get around the car without breaking a heel," Mary said.

"What are you talking about?" all three said in unison.

I use this device quite a lot in writing my humorous stories. It has other applications. Mass confusion in characters is good. It can lead to confrontation, tension and emotional outbursts, all of which will entertain the readers. Mass confusion can also lead to a very funny scene. The Abbott and Costello routine, "*Who's on First*," comes to mind.

First person point of view

In first person POV, the narrator and the POV character are one and the same. The entire story is told from inside the mind of this POV character. The reader can see, hear and learn only what that POV character can see, hear and learn. For this reason the author has to get deep inside the head of this character and has to become quite intimate with the character.

This type of POV is popular with mystery writers and is used in most memoirs.

Unlike third person POV, the author can't switch from a character in Manhattan to a character in San Francisco to explain what's going on out west. The Manhattan character (and the readers) won't know about the events out west unless another character tells him about the event over the phone or the Manhattan character sees it on TV. This limitation implies that the main character has to be present at all major plot events. Having a major plot event take place someplace else won't work. In this instance, the character and the reader learn about it secondhand which is much too distant to hold the reader's interest. To use first person, the plot has to be designed in such a way that the main character is involved at each event as the plot unfolds.

The POV character doesn't have to be the main character. She can be the sidekick who then reports on what the main character is doing. The Sherlock Holmes books are written this way.

First person narratives are extremely personal. The author is telling the story entirely from a single POV and that means uncovering all the character's emotions, his feelings, his dislikes and his biases. At every step, the reader learns the character's motivations and attitudes. The reader must learn why the character acts and reacts the way he does.

This requirement makes first person narratives more difficult to write than third person narratives.

More point of view

Changing point of view characters is often necessary in third person POV. However there is a right way and a wrong way to do the switch.

The best way to change point of view characters is to start a new scene for the new point of view character. Another acceptable way is to start a new paragraph within the same scene. In this case, you have to make sure the new POV character is mentioned in the first line of the new paragraph. If this method of switching is done wrong, the reader will end up with a vast amount of confusion.

The wrong way to switch POV characters is to switch in succeeding sentences. Thus, one sentence uses Jack as the POV character and in the next sentence, Bridget takes over. Then back to Jack. This scenario indicates an inexperienced writer who hasn't mastered the concept of point of view yet.

In my novels, I usually switch POV characters by starting a new scene, but this isn't always possible. In action scenes with multiple characters, I have to switch quickly between these characters to let the reader know what is going on. In these instances I start a new paragraph. Using new scenes won't work here because it would break up the action and slow it down. In a situation with three or four characters and a lot of action, starting new scenes will end up with four, five, even six new scenes instead of one. This many scenes would remove any urgency from the situation and make the encounter drag on until it is no longer interesting, thus the need to use new paragraphs to switch POV characters.

Chapter 12: Writing Voice

Hank Quense: So, you've absorbed all the material on setting, characters, plot and the other stuff. Now you have one more big step to take.

Author: What? More?

*HQ: Yeah. And this is a **very** important step.*

Author: Okay. What is it?

HQ: If you learn only one thing from my book, make it this. You cannot write the way you speak. You have to develop a distinct writing voice, one that is quite different from your speaking voice.

Author: Come on! What's wrong with the way I speak?

HQ: Try this. Eavesdrop on a conversation. One that doesn't involve you or anyone you know.

Author: I'm supposed to learn something from this eavesdropping?

HQ: Uh-huh. What you'll learn is that the conversation is boring to anyone who doesn't know the people involved. You'll also notice that the conversation uses a lot of slang and special ways of talking.

Author: All right, I did it. I overheard a conversation. After a few minutes I lost interest in what they were talking about.

HQ: So, if this conversation in a speaking voice couldn't hold your interest, why would you think an entire book written in a speaking voice won't bore the readers.?

Author: That's an interesting observation. So how do I develop a writing voice and what does it entail?

HQ: I thought you'd never ask. Let's get started.

Was and Were

In any conversation, we use 'was' and 'were' in almost every sentence. While satisfactory for speaking, that makes for boring reading. You have to develop a habit of using alternate verb constructions. Preferably, these verb constructions will use active verbs. This is not easy to do, but it's well worth it. It will vastly improve your writing and that correlates to more reader interest.

Oddly enough, this rule doesn't apply to dialog. Why not, you may ask? It doesn't apply because dialog has to sound natural and that means using 'was' and 'were' a lot. If the characters' dialog doesn't use sentence constructions using 'was' and 'were', the dialog will be stilted and stiff.

Once again I'll emphasize that what I'm talking about is developing a writing voice that is different from your speaking voice and this writing voice must limit "was" and "were" usage to the minimum.

Want to see an example?

With speaking voice:

Larry was cold. He was hungry. He was also tired. He was walking along a muddy road and he was miles from home.

With writing voice:

Larry — cold, hungry and exhausted — slogged along a muddy road miles from home.

I rest my case.

Words ending in -ing

Another facet of many speaking voices is an addiction to -ing words. When used in writing, it gives the material an unpleasant sing-song effect.

Here is an example of what I mean:

With speaking voice:

Opening the door and running down the corridor while waving her hand, she tried shouting, calling attention to her life-threatening situation.

With writing voice:

She opened the door and ran down the corridor. She shouted and waved her hand to call attention to the dangerous situation.

This represents one more element in the development of your writing voice.

Adverbs

Adverbs are a component of our speaking habits and they are one of my pet peeves. I really hate them. So does Stephen King, who once said (or wrote) *"The road to Hell is paved with adverbs."* I actually have an adverb budget. I allocate two or, at the most, three adverbs per five thousand words.

However, I have to admit that my first drafts are studded with adverbs. There is a good reason for this. When writing a first draft, my objective is get the story down on paper as fast as possible. Adverbs are great for this purpose because they are easy to use and allow me to write faster. During the second and third draft, I remove as many adverbs as I possibly can. To do this requires some creativity and heavy thinking. By the time I finish a third or fourth draft, you'll be hard pressed to find an adverb in the story.

Let's look an example.

With speaking voice:

Sara hesitantly entered the room and slowly walked to the reception desk. She smiled wanly at the receptionist and tentatively said her name in a slightly accented voice.

With writing voice:

Sara entered the office and spotted the reception desk. After a slight hesitation, she walked over, smiled and announced her name.

By the way, the examples I use in this chapter aren't completely (adverb!) made up. They're based on stories I critiqued and these stories really (adverb!) did sound like this.

Pronouns

Another feature of the speaking voice is a limitless supply of pronouns. Often the speaker will use several pronouns in a single sentence. Thus, it's not unusual to hear "He said he wasn't doing it no matter what he did." There are three pronouns in the sentence and it's possible that each one refers to a different person. Maybe the folks listening to the speaker wouldn't be confused, but a reader certainly would be.

By itself, this pronoun issue is reason enough to justify the development of a writing voice. And the writing voice has to use names instead of pronouns.

Empty words

In our speaking voices we use empty words. A lot of empty words. The empty words are often substituted for punctuation.

Here is a partial list of empty words we use in speaking: very, even, ever, really, still, just, then. I'm sure you can up with many more. And there's "like" used as comma or in place of a pause.

However, sometimes these words aren't empty. On occasion they actually add meaning to a sentence. How can you tell?

Use the Empty Word Test:

    Step 1) Remove the word from the sentence.
    Step 2) Did the meaning of the sentence change?
    Step 3a) If yes, it's not an empty word. Keep it
    Step 3b) If no, it's an empty word. Remove it.

Naked nouns

While I'm at it, I'll add another annoying writing habit although it isn't a speaking voice issue.

I once critiqued a short story that I found irritating. It wasn't a bad story. It had a good plot and decent characters, but as I read it, I kept getting annoyed by something. Eventually, I figured out what was so annoying. Every noun had one, two and sometimes three adjectives to accompany it. There wasn't a naked noun in the entire story.

Every noun does not have to have a modifier. There is nothing wrong with a naked noun. Here is an example.

The scrawny boy used his undersized biceps to try to pick up the clumsy weight and place it in the old-fashioned truck before the foul-mouthed old man became aware of his clever trickery.

Problem solved:

The boy attempted to pick up the weight and get it into the truck before the old man discovered him.

Horrible example

The example below is a speaking voice taken to the extreme. It's not that far-fetched. I'll bet you've heard people say stuff like this.

In retrospect, I have to say, I had difficulty writing this example. My built-in writing voice kept trying to change it and rewrite it.

Julia was very unhappy with her really bad-tempered aunt and shouted at her just to let her know how really mean she still was. Julia then stamped her blue-and-white sneaker, really hard, and running out of the small room while slamming the brown door very loudly she wondered why old people were so really dumb.

So what's wrong with all these words? They're all perfectly good ones.

I hope the material in this chapter has convinced you of the need to develop a writing voice that is different from your speaking voice.

Part 4: More Stuff

Chapter 13: Parody, Humor and Satire

Hank Quense: In this chapter I'll take you through the process of writing humorous or satiric stories.

Author: Process? Don't you just throw in some jokes and have the characters yell a lot?

HQ: Hmm. I think you watch too many TV sitcoms. Remember, you're writing a story so there won't be a laugh track to tell the readers they just read something funny.

Author: Yeah, no laugh track does complicate things, doesn't it?

HQ: Another important issue is this: you can't write a non-humorous story and after it's finished decide to change it to a humorous story by adding a few jokes. That will never work. The humor has to be built into the design process from the beginning. You have to deliberately set out to create a parody using humor or satire.

Author: Uh-oh. Now you're getting complicated.

HQ: You have to understand the process in order to successfully create parody, humor and satire.

Author: Aren't parody, humor and satire the same things?

HQ: No they are not the same. They are similar, but they have important differences. I use parody to develop the humor and satire in my novels. I'll start by describing parody and then move into the other topics.

Author: You going to explain those differences?

HQ: You betcha.

Parody

Writing humor and satire is difficult. There is a lot more involved than simply dropping in a few joke lines or having a character take a pratfall. The humor or satire has to be integrated into the story design and the writing, not added as an afterthought.

Let's start with a definition of parody. This one is from Wikipedia: *A parody (also called spoof, send-up or lampoon), in use, is a work created to imitate, make fun of, or comment on an original work, its subject, author, style, or some other target, by means of satiric or ironic imitation.*

Also from Wikipedia we have critic Dwight Macdonald offering the general definition: *"Parody is making a new wine that tastes like the old but has a slightly lethal effect."*

My novels are all parodies. Two of these are sci-fi novels. One is a parody of First Contact stories (*Zaftan Entrepreneurs*), and the second is a parody on Space Opera (*Zaftan Miscreants*). In the fantasy genre, I've written parodies on Wagner's *Ring Cycle* of operas (*Wotan's Dilemma*) on Shakespeare (*Falstaff's Big Gamble*) and on Camelot (*Princess Moxie* series).

I consider the subject of the parody, Shakespeare's plays for instance, as the theme of the novel. Once I decide on this theme, some story details fall into place. Many of the characters will be based on whatever topic I'm planning to parody. In *Falstaff's Big Gamble*, it's Hamlet and Othello along with other characters. In *Wotan's Dilemma*, it's Siegfried, Brunnhilde, Fafner, Wotan and others.

In some cases, picking a parody subject will also define the story setting. *Princess Moxie* is a Camelot parody, so the setting is southern Britain in the fourth century. The decision to write a Camelot parody also brought along a number of characters: King Arthur, Guinevere, Lancelot and Merlin to name a few.

Once I have the theme (parody topic) I can move ahead with the story design.

A major part of the problem with writing humor or satire is that humor and satire are very subjective. What one reader will see as hilarious, another will view as stupid. Thus, no matter how good a humor writer you are, you always have the disadvantage that many readers will think your stuff is dumb. While this caveat applies to all writing, it is much more pronounced with humor and satire. More about satire later.

Story basics

In Chapter 1, I used this definition to describe a story:

A story is a narrative description of a character struggling to solve a problem. Nothing more than that. And nothing less. Ben Bova T*he Craft of Writing Science Fiction.*

This definition dictates that the story design must include a protagonist, an antagonist, a plot problem and a plot.

This has been covered before, so why do I repeat it here? Because the humorous story needs all those elements *plus the humor*.

It is always a fatal mistake to believe that just because you're writing a humorous story, you don't need a plot problem or an antagonist or even a plot. I'm appalled at how many stories I've critiqued from newbie writers who substitute humor for a basic story design element. Thus, the so-called humorous story lacks a plot or an antagonist or, in extreme cases, both. Other writers create a basically non-humorous story and add a lot of yelling and shouting by the characters in an effort to generate humor. This is an obvious attempt to emulate TV sitcoms. The yelling accompanied by a laugh track is a common device in TV sitcoms. Alas, it isn't funny on TV and is less funny in a story.

Another basic consideration in writing humorous stories is that the humor must have a target. It has to be focused. The humor (and especially satire) must be aimed at someone or something. Oftentimes, the target will be a byproduct of establishing the theme of the story. Target-less humor will lack a punch while targeted humor is like a slap in the face.

Humor story design

Character building and plot are the story design elements that are used to produce a humorous (or satiric) story.

Let's begin with character development. In this case, the humorous character has to have a bizarre *mental* flaw. The more bizarre the better. Notice, I said *mental* flaw. This doesn't imply a mental handicap. Handicaps, mental and/or physical, are not humorous and attempting to use these handicaps as a source of humor will come across as cruelty, not humor.

The mental flaw in the humorous character makes the character act differently than non-flawed characters in certain situations, usually stressful ones.

The purpose of the plot is to put the flawed character into situations where the flaw stands out, front and center. This flaw dictates how the character acts and reacts in the situation. The flawed character's actions are dramatically different from the way a non-flawed (i.e. normal) character will act.

The best example of a flawed character is Inspector Clouseau from the Pink Panther movies. Clouseau is my idol. When developing a comic character I always use him as a model and I try to emulate him.

Clouseau's flaw is that he thinks he's the world's greatest detective. As such, he can't conceive of ever making a mistake. So when he falls down a flight of stairs into a room full of people, he jumps up and says, "Well, that was refreshing." In another movie, he makes an impassioned speech threatening to unmask the killer, spins on his heel to make a dramatic exit and walks into a wall. Clouseau bounces off the wall, looks at the camera and snarls, "Stupid architect."

In these brief examples, you can see the character's flaw and the plot working together to produce the humor.

To use examples from my own stories, let's look at *Princess Moxie*. In the beginning of this two-book series, Moxie is an obnoxious, whiny teenage brat and she's never been outside her father's castle. Moxie's flaw is that she's noble-born and thinks the purpose of non-noble-born people is to obey her every command and wish.

Moxie is betrothed to a count living far away and her father hires three knights of the Round Table to escort her. Along the way, Moxie is stunned to learn the knights don't care about her noble birth and they ignore her commands. Meanwhile the plot gets the four characters into a host of problems. These include losing the horses, getting attacked by bandits and making a detour to evade Saxon raiders. During these events, Moxie is appalled at the knights disregard for her comfort and wishes. The men go about doing whatever has to be done. Moxie compares their actions with the indecisiveness and busy-work projects within her father's castle. This leads Moxie to introspection and forces her to face the reality of her life up to that point; she's useless and hasn't been trained or educated to do anything.

Slowly, Moxie loses her noble-born fetish which is replaced by a new flaw: her appalling ignorance. She sets out to learn about life and reality, leading to many more humorous situations involving her ignorance of ordinary life.

Another example comes from my Zaftan series of sci-fi novels. I developed a race of aliens who believe that treachery and assassination are social skills. Successful acts are considered resumé material. My main alien character is a female named Klatze who is determined to get ahead on her own ability, a trait so rarely seen it's considered mythical by many other Zaftans. The plot, in this case, gets Klatze into situations where she tries to use her ability instead of murder or at least a degree of violence.

The critical point to be made here is that the plot situations have to be constructed so they are believable to the reader. There has to be an underlying logic to these events. They simply can't be pulled out of a hat and fitted into the story. That won't work. In writing humorous or satiric stories you still have to build a believable plot path through the plot cloud.

Satire

The purpose of satire is different from the purpose of humor. Humor is written to entertain and to make people laugh. Satire does that also, but it has an additional purpose: to make the reader angry. The thing with satire is that it has to have a target that pisses off the author. Satire can't be written by a happy author.

Much satire is time-dependent and doesn't age well because it is aimed at a current situation or personality. A work of satire that is pointed and skews a topical subject will seem dated in a few years (or less), whereas good humor will still be relevant. An example of satire becoming stale is when it is aimed at a politician. It's topical as long as the politician is in office. Once he leaves, the satire becomes dated and isn't relevant any more.

An exception to this out-of-date satire concern is Joseph Heller's *Catch-22*. It is just as fresh and relevant today as it was when originally written. That is because the object of its ridicule, the military bureaucracy, hasn't changed. The Pentagon is just as stuffy and self-important as it was in World War II. Another satiric novel with long legs is *The Vertical Smile* by

Richard Condon. This is perhaps the funniest book I've ever read. In this book, Condon attacks social conditions that haven't changed since the book was published which explains why the satire is still relevant.

I find the structure of *Catch-22* to be a work of art. The first part of the book is ninety percent humor or satire and ten percent horror. Over the course of the novel, this percentage changes to fifty-fifty in the middle and by the end it is ten percent humor or satire and ninety percent horror. At the end of the novel, the reader is enraged. The end of the movie does even a better of job of making the viewer furious.

Deformities and handicaps:

Humor doesn't come from mocking a character's disabilities or deformities. Humor comes from oddball behavior caused by bizarre inner characteristics in one or more of the story's characters, not through their physical appearances.

A writer can use oblique references to get across physical deformities and disabilities without actually describing them. As an example, I used the Wyrd Sisters (from Shakespeare's MacBeth) in a short story. The sisters in my story are middle-aged, ugly and obese, but I never directly mention these features during the story. Instead I mention their tent-sized robes and the panicky reaction of men when they meet the sisters. These reactions tell the reader a lot about how the sisters looked without actually describing them.

Unusual Reactions:

When faced with a situation, humorous characters go to great lengths to react in an unconventional or weird manner. Another aspect of these characters is a wonderful ability to misinterpret information and to arrive at a bizarre conclusion that normal people would never consider. Inspector Clouseau is an example for both of this characteristics.

Omniscient Point of view:

The omniscient point of view is used frequently in humor to get snide remarks and witty observations into the story, but it isn't used to tell the entire story. Rather, the omniscient POV sections are interspersed throughout the work to emphasize the humor. Frequently, these interruptions are used by the author to make cutting remarks on the characters, life, politicians or whatever else is relevant and skew-able.

An interesting aside is the fact that in humor or comedy writing, these interruptions are allowed, even encouraged. In all other types of fiction, the interruptions are considered bad writing because it stops the story from moving forward. These interruptions are also permitted in musical plays. There, the story stops while the characters sing and dance their hearts out. After they finish, the story resumes.

TV Sitcoms:

It is a drastic mistake for an author to imitate TV sit-coms, unless the author is writing a script for one of them. Much of the humor in these shows is generated by shouting or by using visual gags. Shouting or yelling is not humorous by itself. TV uses canned laughter to let the viewers know they are supposed to laugh. Thus, the non-humorous shouting and yelling is accompanied by canned laughter to make sure the viewer realizes a joke just occurred. Without the laugh track, the viewers wouldn't notice the so-called joke.

Likewise, visual gags are difficult to translate into written humor. If you are serious about writing humor, I advise you to avoid watching TV sit-coms.

A different attempt by movie and TV to add humor is to have a character use insults or foul language at every opportunity. This has a certain shock value initially, but it quickly grows stale and, after a short time, becomes irritating rather than humorous.

Chapter 14: Odds and Ends

Hank Quense: We're getting close to the end of the book. Before we finish up, I have a few more topics to cover.
Author: This stuff seems endless.
HQ: Patience, grasshopper. The end is in sight and the material in this chapter is important.
Author: You say that about every chapter.
HQ: Well, it all is important.
Author: Okay. Bring it on.
HQ: That's the spirit.

World building
Many sci-fi and fantasy authors build new worlds for their characters to romp around in. These worlds are complicated structures that require a lot of hard work and creativity. These writers then feel compelled to share their creations with the reader and they go overboard in describing their world. This need to share information results in page after page of exposition with in-depth details of the geography, the solar system, the ecology, the plant and animal life. Possibly the author will even include the history of intelligent life on the world, all fifty million years of it.

Many readers relish this type of detail, but unfortunately most readers don't need to know most of these details in order to enjoy the story. They are willing to assume the author's wonderful world works just fine without learning detailed knowledge of it. They just want to get back to the story.

Granted a reader does need to know something of the worlds in order to keep up their suspension of belief, but the amount of information required is much less than the author assumes the readers need.

To hold the readers' interest, the world-building information should be limited to that which is absolutely necessary. That means the reader doesn't have to know how Mount Hogwash came to be 6,257 feet high. It also means the relevant information should be dispensed in small, easily digested paragraphs that don't stop the action, unlike the long passages of exposition that are often used.

This is one more instance where the author has to suppress his ego and put the needs of the reader first.

Copyrights and rights
Under US law, everything you write is automatically copyrighted without your doing anything specific about it. This applies to stories, memoirs, shopping lists and the to-do lists stuck on your refrigerator. In other words,

your manuscript is protected by law and no one can reproduce, print or distribute your work unless you grant them permission to do so.

There are methods to strengthen your copyright protection by registering the work with the Library of Congress. I've never thought that was necessary since I doubt anyone would want to steal my work. The Library of Congress process involves fees. You can learn more by following this link: http://www.copyright.gov.

I prefer to rely on the the copyright symbol © to warn folks to stay away. Use it like this: Copyright © 2016 by Hank Quense. Naturally, use your name, not mine. You don't have to add the symbol to shopping lists.

Rights are different from copyrights. "Rights" are something you, the author, can grant to another party. There are a number of types of rights and all of them grant differing permissions to the other party. There is an excellent article written by Moira Allen who runs the *Writing World* website. Here is a link: http://www.writing-world.com/rights/copyright.shtml. You should read this article and bookmark it or print it. Refer to it whenever a publisher or someone else wants to acquire the rights to something you wrote.

Stolen Manuscripts

In my lectures, I'm often asked if I have any concerns about my work getting stolen when I send it to an editor or a beta reader or to a publisher. The person asking the question always has real concerns about this issue. This question mostly comes from writers who have no publication credits and usually have never submitted anything because of their fear of thievery.

I make two comments by way of response. First, these writers are assuming their work is good enough to be worth stealing. However, since they haven't had anything published in a paying market, they have no basis to make that assumption. Second, why would anyone steal the work of an unknown, unpublished writer? That doesn't make sense.

I don't know of any published writer or author who has the least concern about their unpublished work getting stolen by an editor. Published authors and writers are concerned about the piracy of their published works, but that is an entirely different issue.

In Conclusion

If you've made this far in the book and you're new to fiction writing, your head is probably aswirl with all the information and concepts you're expected to master. DO NOT PANIC! You don't have to master all this stuff in one sitting.

The best way to approach this material is just start writing. Create a story and work up the characters and the plot as best you can. As you create more stories, your characters will become better and your plots more intricate and believable. It takes time to become adept at story design and story-telling.

Along with writing, you should read. Read a lot. Don't just read for entertainment. Examine how the author describes his characters and the settings and the plot twists. Feel free to emulate the author when you un-cover a neat writing trick.

To conclude, reading and writing are the keys to mastering the materi-al in this book. *You can do it!* But understand there is no fiction-pill you can swallow to make it easy. It will take time and effort.

Chapter 15: Other Stuff

Hank Quense: We're approaching the end.
Author: Finally!
HQ: The material in this chapter is optional.
Author: What does that mean?
HQ: You don't have to read it, but I urge you to give it a try. It could save you a lot of aggravation by showing you alternative ways to organize your work.
Author: Okay. I'll give a shot as long as I don't have to commit to using the stuff.
HQ: What a guy!

Mind-mapping a story

Developing a long story is a complex undertaking. There are a myriad of details involved. Remembering all of them, or even where the details are filed, is difficult. I've developed a solution that works for me: mind-maps.

I'm not prepared to start writing the first draft until I have a complete set of mind-maps at hand. This involves developing a set of three (minimum) mind-maps. One is for the characters and shows their major details. I described the character mind-map in Chapter 5. In this chapter, I'll describe two additional mind-maps. One is for the plot and the second is a graphical synopsis. Developing this last one is, in effect, a test to make sure I completely understand the novel I'm about to write. If I can complete the graphical synopsis I'm ready to write the story.

Let's go through the mind-maps one at a time. If you are revolted by the idea of creating a mind-map, you may want to skip this section. For the record, I find this type of planning to be fun.

Plot mind-maps

Since novels are large, complex undertakings, it follows that the mind-maps will also be large and complex. The points I'm trying to make will be swallowed up by the size and complexity of these mind-maps if I use a novel in the explanation. So I've come up with a way to simplify the demonstration. *Wotan's Dilemma* is short novel (a novella really) with four acts and a small cast. The acts are named after a series of operas and the plot mind-map for the first act is shown below. This mind-map displays the main plot events in the opening act of the story.

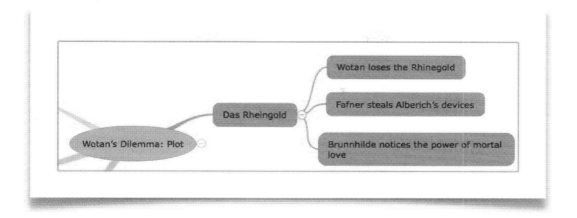

The complete mind-map for *Wotan's Dilemma* is shown below. It details the plot events for all four acts.

I don't expect the details will be understandable to readers who aren't familiar with the novel, but the picture illustrates the ability of the mind-map to present a complicated plot in its entirety.

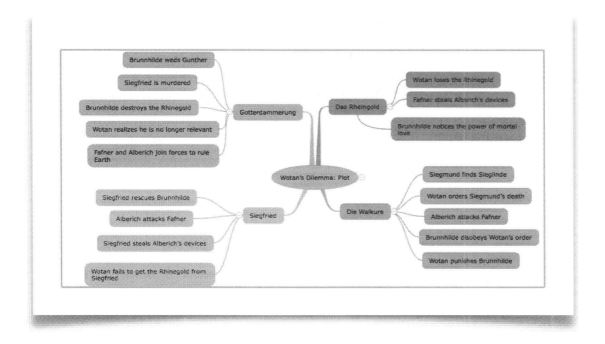

Graphical Synopsis

This is my most important mind-map. It's the one I look at the most. It's also the most complicated and the most time-consuming to construct, but I think the effort is worth it. In this mind-map, I depict the major activities for each character in each act.

Here is a brief synopsis of *Wotan's Dilemma* so the mind-map will make more sense. In my version of this ancient myth, Brunnhilde is a Valkyrie (a minor goddess). She is the main character and she discovers that mortal love is more powerful then any of the gods ever imagined. Wotan is the chief god and his power and immortality rest on possessing the Rhinegold, a magical horde of gold.

The original myth contains dwarfs and a dragon, but I changed them to aliens for my version. Their names are Fafner and Alberich. Alberich acquires the Rhinegold and Fafner steals it from Alberich. Wotan has to get it back from Fafner or he and all the gods are doomed.

Wotan creates a mortal, Siegmund, whose job it is to father Siegfried, a great hero who will kill Fafner, take the Rhinegold and give it to Wotan. At least that what Wotan hopes will happen. It doesn't.

To start the synopsis mind-map I create the central idea bubble, *Wotan's Dilemma*: Synopsis. I then add child bubbles for each main character and add sub-children corresponding to each of the four acts.

Next, I add the rest of the cast. This makes the mind-map rather large. The ability to show each character in a different color is a useful tool that simplifies reading the mind-map.

To finish the synopsis, I then add the activities and/or events for the rest of the characters in each act. I won't attempt to display that version of the mind-map here. It's quite large and detailed, but it allows me to control the development of the book.

Below is Brunnhilde's portion of the map along with the rest of the cast.

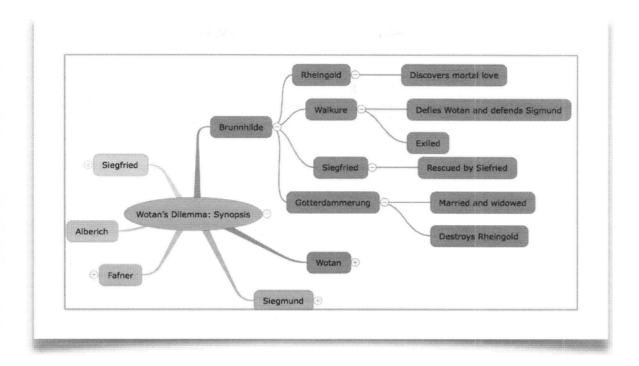

While you may be appalled at the thought of spending time developing a mind-map like this, think about the usefulness of it. Brunnhilde's story is depicted here. The map shows what happens to her in each act and simplifies the writing of the story by furnishing me with a guide for each step of the novel.

These maps aren't static in that they are not unchangeable. As the novel progresses, changes inevitably occur and the changes require that the mind-maps be updated.

The graphical synopsis can also be used to sanity-check the journey of each character. Does Brunnhilde's story make sense? Is there a gaping hole in the plot events she is involved in? Does the Wotan-Brunnhilde conflict make sense?

In summary, I find mind-mapping a novel to be a necessary step in the development of the story design. You may think the graphical synopsis is overkill (I don't); you may also see the advantages of developing a mind-map for your characters.

Scrivener

In writing a story, many authors use a word processor and end up with a great many small files on their hard drive. There are character write-ups, plot notes, sketches of locations and research notes to name a few. Perhaps every scene is a separate file. Chapters may be another set of files. All of these files with their obscure file names make it difficult to retrieve information when you need it. Rearranging scenes and chapters under these conditions becomes a herculean task.

The solution to this problem is to use a writing program. The one I use is Scrivener. Personally, I would never attempt to write a book, fiction or non-fiction, without Scrivener. This book was put together with Scrivener. The program is large and has many features that I don't use, or even know about. I probably use less than forty percent of the features. With each new book I write, I discover one or more additional features which I then start to use.

Scrivener can be used to write anything. Besides fiction and non-fiction books (it has prebuilt templates for both) it can also be used to write scripts or plays. Students can use it to write theses and reports.

Scrivener is my go-to program for writing books. With Scrivener, you have a single file that contains everything (literally!) about the story you're writing. There are sections to hold scenes, chapters, character sketches, plot information, notes, location sketches, and anything else you can think of, including my mind-maps. Another interesting feature is that each scene (and other information) can be tagged as first draft, second draft, final, etc. The program has no length limitations. I've used it for four-thousand-word short stories and for eighty-thousand word novels. I also use it for writing articles and non-fiction books.

The bigger the project the more valuable Scrivener is. It also has an excellent support structure. On its website, there are blogs, forums, videos and a lot of other information.

Granted there is a learning curve when you first start using Scrivener, but there are excellent tutorials to get you started. These tutorials are part of the program. My approach was to learn enough to get me writing my book and learn additional features on the fly. I'm sure that there are many features I'll never need, so why bother to learn them?

Below is a screen shot from one of my novels.

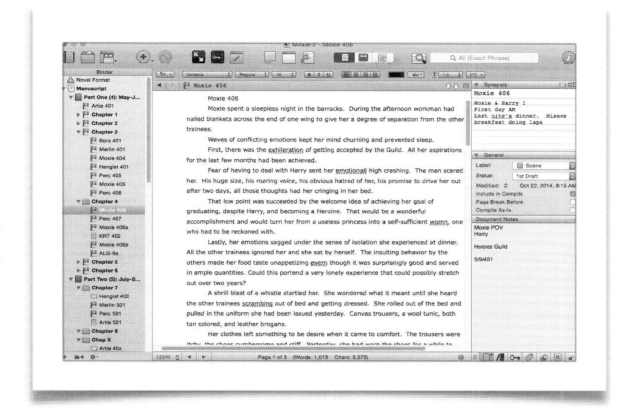

The long list on the left shows the scenes in the story grouped by chapter. I use different colored flags to indicate the status of the scene or chapter. Scenes and chapters with a green flag are a second draft while the blue flags indicate a first draft. Scenes without a flag haven't been written yet.

The text in the middle is the scene I'm currently working on. On the right is meta-data. On the top is a brief synopsis of the scene. In the yellow area on the bottom right, I list the cast of characters in the scene along with which one is the POV character, the location of the scene and the date of the scene in story time.

Part of the problem with long stories is remembering what you said in earlier scenes or recalling whether a character has a full head of hair or is partially bald. This is especially true if the character hasn't been in a recent scene. Scrivener makes it easy to find the information you need since that information is only one or two mouse clicks away.

Another advantage with Scrivener is the ease of rearranging scenes and chapters. If I wish to move a scene from chapter ten to chapter three, all I have to do is click on the scene in the left part of the screen and drag it between chapters. Try doing that with a word processor document with all its small files. Scrivener and word processors are completely different animals. Once you finish the story (after many drafts) you can tell Scrivener to export it in a variety of formats including Epub and Word.

My way
I have my own way of developing a story. I don't think of it as unique; I'm sure other authors have a similar process. I believe in doing ALL of the design work prior to writing a first draft. This includes any research that may be required. In the case of my novel, *Falstaff's Big Gamble* — a Shakespearian parody — I tracked how long it took me to complete this design work. From the time I had a brainstorm and figured out the ending and how to develop the story, I spent three months working on the design. This entailed developing a number of characters (six main characters and about a dozen minor ones), coming up with the plot lines (three major plots and three subplots) and the setting (a fantasy country called Gundarland).

After the three months, I spent more time developing the mind-maps I'd use prior to writing the first draft. That took another week or two.

Here is a graphic I use in my lecture on creating fiction. I use it to explain my way of getting the design work done.

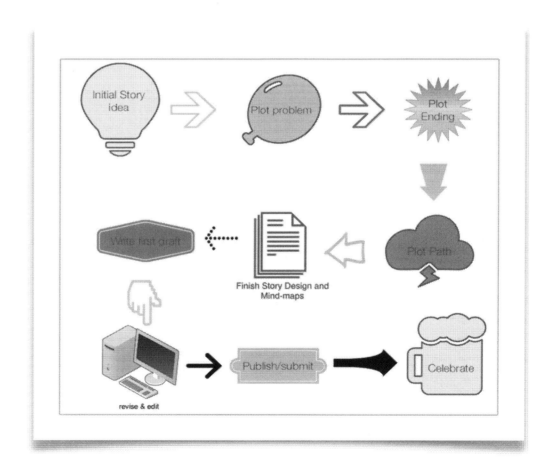

My initial idea for a story always starts with a character. Your story could start that way or with a plot problem idea or even a setting. The point is, one way isn't better than the others. All are equally valid.

My overall story setting usually comes with the character. For instance, if the initial character is a dwarf, obviously, the overall story setting is some sort of fantasy land. If the character is an alien, a sci-fi story will ensue.

My next step is to figure out what big plot problem the character will have to solve. Along with this, I need to come up with a motivation for the character. Why does the character need/want to solve this problem. It's possible for the character to say, "Screw this. I'm not wasting my time on this dumb problem." This has happened to me. (Dealing with uppity characters is one of the drawbacks of writing fiction). Basically, the character is telling me I need a new problem. If I force the character to work on this problem against his will, he won't be happy and neither will the reader who will see though the fake motivation I gave the character.

So, I have a character, a setting and a plot problem. That isn't too difficult to achieve, but the next step is very hard. I concentrate on coming up with the plot ending, the story's climax in other words. This is a make or break situation. If I can't come up with the ending, the story idea gets scrapped or at least filed under "Someday". I don't develop the characters or do anything else with the story until I get the ending. I may come up with ideas such as situations or bits of dialog that I'll write down and save, but that's incidental work. I need the ending and I'm not wasting time on other development work until I get one.

The next step is to test the idea to see if it is a valid climax. It may turn out, upon inspection, to be too trivial to use. Then it's back to the starting point. I need another ending.

Once I have a valid ending, I move on to the next design step: connecting the beginning of the story with the climax, also not an easy task. This process is described in Chapter 6. Oftentimes, here too, I'll get a plot path that won't yield a satisfactory process. The path can be silly, ludicrous, or even too stupid to even consider. Then I have to figure out another plot path.

After I have a climax and a solid plot path (i.e. one that I can believe in), I start developing the characters in the story. Once the cast is complete, I finally start on the mind-maps followed by first draft and the other tasks in the diagram.

One of the advantages of planning a long story this way involves the idea generation that results from it. The act of developing characters, plots, settings, scenes and other details will trigger ideas about the characters and the other elements. It may be a snippet of dialog. It may be a cool place to use for a scene. Or it could be an interesting plot twist. Whatever it is, I write it down for possible use. I once estimated that a novel requires more than a hundred good ideas. Now, I think that number is way too low for a novel. You need ideas on characters, plot events, setting, scene locations and a myriad of other topics. The earlier you start collecting these ideas, the better off you and your story will be. If you don't plan your story beforehand, sooner or later you'll have to stop writing to search for ideas.

Chapter 16: Appendices

In this chapter, I have an assortment of unrelated topics. First up, I took a scene from one of my short stories and annotated it to illustrate the scene design development. A second topic is a list of books on writing that I consider to be worth the money to acquire and keep on hand. Lastly, I put a copy of my character development sheet. You can copy it and keep it on your computer to use while working on new stories.

Annotated scene
Romeo & Juliet (C) 2010
Author's note: This is a scene from a short story published originally in *Tales From Gundarland*. I've annotated it to highlight the scene design concepts.

~ ~ ~

Romeo thought his shift would never end. It was the longest night he had ever experienced. Finally, it ended and he cleaned up. Gulping large draughts of air because of his excitement and anticipation, he ran to the Capulet house in the wealthy part of town. He paused outside the garden to listen for signs of the brothers.

Setting details: late at night, Juliet's garden
Scene Goal: To get laid
Initial emotion: high level of anticipation

After a few minutes of silence he scaled the wall and dropped down on the other side. He landed on a laurel shrub, making more noise than he would have liked.

My bad: poor writing here: I should have used more sensory info: cracking limbs, rustling leaves and described a pointy branch sticking him in the leg

He moved away from the wall. The garden had so many trees, it resembled a forest, and the leaves whispered in a light breeze.

Sensory information: hearing

"Romeo, Romeo, wherefore art thou Romeo?"

Juliet awaited him!

"Hsst. I'm over here, caught on a thorn bush." He tugged his cloak and felt it rip, but he was free. He hastened to her.

Juliet wore a diaphanous nightgown and her lithe beauty stood revealed in the light of a three-quarter moon. Romeo skidded to a halt at the sight of her. He stood, drinking in her magnificence. She smiled and held out her arms. He skipped forward and they embraced. Giddy with love and lust, he undid the buttons in front of his face. He parted the cloth, inhaled her essence, coughed and spit out a gobbet of belly-button lint.

Sensory information: taste
"Oh my love," Romeo implored. "Say you'll marry me."
"Yes, yes. I'll be rid of the Capulet name forever."
His hands caressed her body.
Sensory information: feel, touch
"What's in a name?" she continued. "That which we call a rose, by any other name would smell as sweet."
"What are you talking about? Have you been snorting funny herbs?" Romeo paused in his explorations. "What's this?"
"My chastity belt." Juliet sighed. "Dreadmona keeps the key on a chain around her neck. And she's very snippy when I wake up her at night to go to the outhouse. As if it was my fault."
Disappointed, but still keen, he explored higher. "Oww!"
"That's my chastity bra. It has a lot of nasty sharp points that always ruin my clothes."
Anticipation is dropping fast
Her hands did their own exploring. "Oh! You have one too?"
"No. That's just my iron cup. I wear it in the mines for protection in case I trip. I forgot to take it off. And it's awfully uncomfortable right now."
She looked down at him. "What are we to do, my darling? My wedding to Count Paris grows nigh."
"I have an idea." He snapped his fingers. "My cousin is a locksmith. Tomorrow night I'll return with a set of master keys. Then we'll become dwarf and wife."
Initial high emotional state is completely deflated.
He embraced her and reluctantly took a step backward. He had to get rid of his cup and find a bucket of cold water. Fast.
"Parting is such sweet sorrow."
"Eh?"
Closing emotion: Depressed

Further Reading
Characters and Viewpoints, Orson Scott Card, Writer's Digest Books. Viewpoint is difficult for a beginning writer to fathom. This book has sketches that visually demonstrate the various viewpoints. An essential book for the writer's library shelf.
Conflict, Action and Suspense, William Noble, Writer's Digest Books. This book concentrates on how to keep the tension high in order to hold the reader's interest.
Creating Short Fiction, Damon Knight, St Martin's Press. Written by a master of fiction writing, this book has lots of good pointers and techniques to help a writer build stories.

Handbook of Short Story Writing, edited by Frank A. Dickson and Sandra Smythe, Writer's Digest

Handbook of Short Story Writing Volume II, edited by Jean M. Fredette, Writer's Digest

Writing to the Point, Algis Budrys. The best (and shortest) book on fiction writing I own. Alas, It is out of print and no longer available.

Plot, Ansen Dibell, Writer's Digest Books. A good book on how to develop a plot.

Self-Editing for Fiction Writers, Renni Browne and Dave King, Harper Perennial. A must-have book for authors. Filled with information on how to improve your stories and your writing skills.

Story, Robert McKee, Regan Books. A thick, excellent book on writing fiction by a master screen writer teacher. As McKee points out, screenplays, stage plays and novels all have the same story design process and problems; only the output (the manuscript) in each is formatted differently.

The Elements of Style, William Strunk and E.B. White, Macmillan Publishing Company. What do you mean you're a writer and you don't already own this one? (or a similar book)

Building Believable Characters, Marc McCutcheon, Writer's Digest Books. Unlike the others on this list, this one isn't a how-to book; it is reference book filled with descriptions you can use to build unique characters.

Character development sheet

You can highlight and copy the information below. Stash it on your computer as a master file so you can duplicate whenever you start developing a new character. Modify it to your heart's content.

Name:
Story Function:
Dominant Reader Emotion(s):

Central Metaphor:

Physical Description:

Biographical Material:

Individual Philosophy:

Individualization Traits:

Descriptor:

Personality:

Type:

Positive traits:

Negative traits:

Dress Habits:

Dialog:

Character Arc:

Motivation:

Memories that influence those motives:

Mirages that the character fools themselves into believing:

About the Author

And now, a few words about the guy who writes this stuff, Hank Quense.

Of late, Hank has been bouncing between fiction novels and non-fiction. Since writing fiction is fun and non-fiction is work, he's dedicating himself to fiction for a while.

On the non-fiction front, Hank has written two series of ebooks. His *Fiction Writing Guides* are aimed at beginning and inexperienced fiction writers. The *Self-publishing Guides* describe the process of publishing and marketing a book.

His *Fiction Writing Guides* consist of *Creating Stories* and *Manage Your Story Design Project* and *Planning a Novel, Script or Memoir*. The first named book concerns itself on fiction writing while the second uses a project management type approach to creating stories. The third is new and describes a process that will enable an author to get control of a long work.

The *Self-publishing Guides* are a set of four books aimed at authors who need to understand the publishing processes. The book titles are: *Self-publishing a Book, Marketing Plans for Self-published Books, Manage Your Self-publishing Project* and *Business Basics for Authors*.

There is also a boxed set incorporating all four titles under a single cover. It's called the *Complete Self Publishing Guide*.

On the fiction front, Hank has written and published a number of parodies. If you enjoy humorous and satiric fantasy and sci-fi fiction, you'll enjoy reading his books. You can chose from:

Zaftan Entrepreneurs

Zaftan Miscreants
Falstaff's Big Gamble
Wotan's Dilemma
Tales From Gundarland

Better yet, why bother choosing. Get a copy of all of them and lay in a supply of laughter.

Links? You want links? Here you go:

Strange Worlds Publishing: http://strangeworldspublishing.com/wp

Hank's blog pages: https://http://hank-quense.com/wp

Hank's Facebook fiction page:
https://www.facebook.com/StrangeWorldsOnline?ref=hl

Hank's Facebook non-fiction page:
151
https://www.facebook.com/pages/Strange-Worlds-Online-Non- fiction/439722529522496?ref=hl

Twitter: https://twitter.com/hanque99